The RightMan Business Plan *for* Women

A business approach to relationships for successful, sassy women!

By RonWilliams

ISBN 978-0-9851620-1-6

Look for The Right Man Business Plan Seminar coming to a location near you. For more information visit: www.therightmanbusinessplan.com

ACKNOWLEDGMENTS

To undertake the task of writing a book takes a combination of motivation and inspiration. I am blessed to have both from my family. This book is really about relationships. Through my parents, I have been able to see, up close and personal, the greatest relationship and expression of love that there is between two people. I want to thank Robert and Joan Williams for being the living picture of what friendship, companionship, caring, kindness, consideration, and affection looks like. To see you two is to witness love in action.

I want to thank my children, Renaldo, Renae, and Rachel, for making me proud of each of you. You three are the wind beneath my wings.

A special thanks to Gail Edmonds, Sr. Copy Editor at ProofreadPlease.com for the tireless and relentless effort it took to copyedit this manuscript.

I wish to express deep appreciation to Paulette Brown, my social media manager, who saw something in this labor of love from the very beginning. Her belief in me, along with the vision she had for this book, has been a source of strength and encouragement.

I owe a profound thank you to the entire The Right Man Business Plan Team, which includes Paulette Brown, Tammy Wright, Earth Angel Public Relations + Marketing Agency, Jackie Mohair, Reiko Clark, and Cookie Wiggins. Your patience and professionalism was outstanding.

3

I am also grateful for the many people who took the surveys, answered questions, and shared their relationship experiences that helped with my research for the book.

My grandmother Rebie Williams, who passed away at 102 years old, always said that everyone has a book in them. At the tender age of 75, she wrote *Louisiana Love* and a few years later penned *Bayou Road*. She was a phenomenal lady and always will be an inspiration and role model.

As a product of my environment—including family, friends, preachers, and teachers—I want to thank all of these influences for helping shape me into the man I have become. However, none of this could be possible without my Lord and Savior Jesus Christ, who has carried me through life's trials and tribulations.

CONTENTS

ACKNOWLEDGMENTS 3

INTRODUCTION 7

CHAPTER 1 – **BUSINESS MEETS ROMANCE** 9

CHAPTER 2 – **QUALITY IS JOB1** 27

CHAPTER 3 – **RELATIONSHIP STAGES** 57

CHAPTER 4 – **MEETING NEEDS** 85

CHAPTER 5 –**RELATIONSHIP ECONOMICS** 101

CHAPTER 6 – **STRATEGIC DATING** 117

CHAPTER 7 –**YOU ARE THE PRODUCT** 159

CHAPTER 8 – **STRUCTURING THE RELATIONSHIP** 195

CHAPTER 9 – **FOUR FACES OF EVE** 215

CHAPTER 10 – **RISKY BUSINESS** 233

CHAPTER 11 – **LEARN FROM THE PAST** 261

CHAPTER 12 – **RELATIONSHIP STRATEGY** 279

CHAPTER 13 – **MARKET PLAN** 289

CHAPTER 14 –**THE PLAN** 339

INTRODUCTION

The premise of this book is to use fundamental business principles and entrepreneurial skills to help successful, sassy, and single females find the right man and have a quality relationship. Normally, when a person authors a book, they are considered a subject matter expert for the topic about which they are writing. An expert is a person with extensive knowledge or ability, predicated on research, experience, or occupation in a particular area of study; they have experience through practice and education. Based on these criteria, I qualify as an expert in the two domains I am writing about in this book: business and relationships.

My expertise in the business domain stems from working in corporate America for 25 years. I have been a President, Vice President, General Manager, Director, Regional Manager, and Sales Rep. I have worked for large companies, small companies, start-up companies, and start-over companies. I have been in the corporate headquarters as well as regional and field offices. I have hired people, fired people, trained people, and developed people.

In addition, I have been in sales, marketing, promotions, advertising, human resources, and training and development. For the past 10 years, I have owned my own business and have worked in both the private sector and with the federal government. I have negotiated both large and small contracts. My business has been certified as a Minority Business Enterprise (MBE), as well as a Small Business Administration Development Program [8(a)]. I have coached, trained, counseled, and advised top executives in the C-suite as well as in the field. I have facilitated and led meetings dealing with strategic planning, key account strategies, gaining market share, reductions in work force, succession planning, and mergers and acquisitions. I know how to start, run, and grow a business.

The second domain, in which I qualify as an expert, is in relationships, both business and romantic. My knowledge comes from extensive research and experience. I was married for 23 years and have been divorced for 10. I have dated and been a member of online dating sites, including eHarmony, Match.com, and Black People Meet. My dating resume includes younger, successful, confident, low self-esteem, aggressive, passive, sensual, sexual, celibate, religious, Black, White, Latina, highly educated, nondegreed, fit, beautiful, plain, average, fabulous women.

I have experienced relationship highs and lows, partners I thought I had a future with; as well as ones that I knew were doomed from the start. I have listened actively to women share their man problems and wiped tears from the cheeks of family members and friends who loved and lost. Over the course of the nine-month preparation to write this book, I have read books, blogs, magazines, articles, tweets, and almost any and everything that had to do with relationships, romance, intimacy, and love. I have surveyed scores of women to hear firsthand their opinions about relationships and dating. Most importantly, I have observed the greatest relationship model anyone could ever have—my parents, who for over 60 years have demonstrated what true love is and what a loving relationship should be.

CHAPTER ONE
BUSINESS MEETS ROMANCE

NOT JUST ANOTHER RELATIONSHIP BOOK

The Right Man Business Plan is not just another relationship book telling you how to find a mate, but rather one that is based on business principles, relationship economics, and entrepreneurial skills. The combination of business knowledge and relationship strategies makes strange bedfellows; but the truth is that they have much in common. The pages of this book will share the similarities and parallels of business and romance. You not only will learn what it takes to start a business, but also you will learn ways to think differently about relationships and what is required to make them lasting and loving.

You will also learn ways to inspect what you expect when it comes to choosing a quality partner. I assure you, if you take the time to honestly answer the assessment questions, follow the processes, and adhere to the principles in this book, you will be amazed and excited by what you learn about yourself and relationships. You will find yourself systematically reviewing aspects of your past partners and relationships, while learning new ways of finding, attracting, and retaining the right life partner.

Many businesses, and the entrepreneurs who start them, are unsuccessful because they are in either the wrong industry or doing the wrong work. Many relationships, and the people who start them, fail because they are with the wrong partner.

The true start-up of a business or a relationship is what happens before you start up. An essential component to business or relationship success is the planning and preparation to lay the proper foundation. Without a solid foundation, no business or relationship is built to last.

The four cornerstones for building a solid foundation in business or relationships are:

- **Vision.** There are two important days in your life—the day you were born and the day you knew why you were born. What do you want your life to be about? What's the big picture? If you don't know where you're going, how will you get there? A vision is having a mental picture of the business or relationship you intend on having.

- **Strategy.** You have to establish what it is you have that would make your customer want to buy from you. What are the things you need to concentrate on for your vision to become a reality? Setting specific goals helps in creating a strategy.

- **Plan.** What steps will you take to achieve your goals? The plan helps to know you have covered all the bases. It is your blueprint for success. Planning allows you to think through the why, what, when, where, and how aspects of business or relationships.

- **Accountability.** When you typically initiate an action plan or goal, what keeps you motivated, challenged, and engaged? Establishing metrics will assist in determining if you are achieving your goals.

ARE YOU SUCCESSFUL AND SASSY?

What makes a modern-day woman successful? This is a woman whose power comes from maintaining control of herself, not relinquishing that control to anyone else. She has overcome adversity and difficult times to consistently provide the needed resources for herself and her family. Her pursuit of professional and personal growth and development has inspired her to accept different challenges, acquire new skills, and expand her networks. While achieving her own goals, she feels the need and urgency to support and help other women achieve their goals. Successful does not mean she has to work in a corporate environment or hold a title. Successful does mean enterprising and striving to better herself in all facets of life. This woman can pass the mirror test, which means she can look at herself and feel good about what she sees. She is someone who knows what she wants out of life, knows what is important in life, and is willing to pay the price to get out of life what she desires and deserves.

What makes a contemporary woman sassy? This ·self-confident, opinionated, and witty woman walks to the beat of her own drum and refuses to let someone else accelerate her pace and rhythm. Her power comes from her strong sense of self. She is both fun and funny and recognizes the strength in her femininity. She lives in the moment; this ambitious assured woman works hard and plays hard. It is not that she is fearless, but she does not let fear stop her from moving forward. She is not afraid of failure, but she is afraid of not living life to its fullest. She wakes up in the morning feeling victorious rather than defeated. Challenges get her competitive juices flowing, and her philosophy is "you don't win the silver, you lose the gold."

NEW APPROACH TO AN AGE-OLD PROBLEM

Observing, hearing about, and knowing many women who were doing well professionally, but not doing as well romantically (including my two beautiful daughters), I came to the conclusion that this was a problem and a solution was required. I realized that if these women continued to do what they have always done concerning dating and relationships, then they would always get what they always have–and that would be insanity. If you want something you have never had, then you have to do things you have never done.

Most women have never looked at dating and relationships like a business. In the pages of this book, you will find similarities between business and romance and learn how to utilize business principles to initiate and maintain a healthy, harmonious relationship.

The success rate for both small businesses and romantic relationships is not very favorable. Statistics show that 95 percent of small businesses fail within the first 5 years of operation and more than half of marriages end in divorce. What these numbers reflect is having a successful business or a successful relationship is not easy.

Nobody wants his or her business or relationship to fail. That is why it is essential that you have a clear understanding of what it is you are trying to achieve and be able to identify challenges and barriers that stand in the way.

Does this mean I am taking the wanderlust and the serendipitous possibilities out of dating and relationships and turning them into a corporate, cold, and calculating formula-based process? Absolutely not; this is a new approach to an age-old problem.

By applying business principles and entrepreneurial skills to romance, you will:

- Enhance your knowledge, which is the what to do.
- Learn new skills, which is the how to do.
- Increase your motivation, which is the want to do.

By positively influencing you in the way you perceive, understand, and interpret relationships, this book will help you make better decisions and choices when it comes to love and romance.

I wrote this book for single women, not for married women; so my advice is geared to someone who is not legally or morally bound to a partner. However, if a married woman reads the book and adopts some of the principles, I hope it improves the quality of the marriage. Similarly, I believe if men choose to read the book, they, too, could learn some things that would help them become better partners.

SELF-LOVE, SELF-ESTEEM, SELF-KNOWLEDGE

Wisdom is best manifested in its simplicity; if things are too complicated, they get lost in translation. This book will be very easy to follow and understand, because the emphasis is on three key things:

1. First key thing is you. Chances are if you are reading this book, you have experienced a bad relationship. Are you ready for a serious relationship; have you healed and recovered from these experiences, or are you still haunted by the terrible twins (trauma and drama)? Some women have decided that they are not emotionally healthy enough or believe they are

undeserving of having a healthy relationship. This book encourages thinking about the prospects of a future positive relationship rather than basing decisions on failed past relationships. Time alone will not get you ready for your next relationship. The things that will help include working on being emotionally available, allocating time to date, and having the determination to create a lasting, loving relationship. This book assists you in knowing your values, priorities, boundaries, strengths, weaknesses, opportunities, threats, nonnegotiable standards, and what you want and need from a partner and a relationship. Self-love, self-esteem, and self-knowledge are necessities for a successful relationship.

2. Second is finding the right partner. The right partner is someone whom you like, trust, respect, and who is a great friend. The right partner will enjoy spending time with you and is compatible. This book helps you know what to look for in a partner; know what to avoid in a partner; understand the male ego; learn what men want; as well as how to find men, attract them, and keep them.

3. Third is developing a healthy relationship. In order to move forward in establishing healthy relationships, you must figure out your relationship patterns and what exactly went wrong in your past relationships. This book helps you to 1) understand what a healthy relationship is and how to develop one, 2) understand how to avoid dating pitfalls, 3) establish relationship strategies, 4) learn the four

stages of relationships, and 5) develop structure profiles.

A healthy, mutually rewarding relationship is so much about knowing who you are and staying on that path. A strong sense of self makes your actions, reactions, and interactions consistent and dependable; which in turn make men feel more comfortable in approaching you and wanting to get to know you.

The wise woman has a philosophy; a philosophy is a set of rules to guide your life and your thought process. Here are 10 wise things to remember as you read this book:

1. **A healthy relationship is like a pair of socks; you have to have two and they have to match.** Look for a man who shares your vision and values, likes to do things you enjoy, and will let you use the remote control. Remember: Opposites don't attract, equals attract.

2. **Most men are not worth crying over, but once you find one who is, he won't make you cry.** Love shouldn't hurt. If your man makes you cry, it may be time to say bye-bye. Remember: look for a man who brings you joy, peace, fun, and laughter.

3. **If he isn't a wind in your sail, then he is an anchor on your tail—cut him loose.** You need a man who is supportive, a positive influence, someone with whom you can share your dreams. Remember: Dreams don't die, someone usually kills them; and some of the best dream killers are called "boyfriends."

15

4. **When the character of a man is not clear to you, look at his friends.** A man is the average of his five closest friends; if he hangs with dirt, he's bound to be dirty; and if he runs with dogs, then he's got fleas. Remember: Penitentiaries are full of good people who had bad friends.

5. **The chains of habit are sometimes too weak to be felt, until they are too strong to be broken.** You are a creature of habit, but some of those habits are hurting you when it comes to men and relationships. If you cannot stop, change, or start a habit when you want to, then you are not in control of it, it is in control of you. Remember: If you always do, what you've always done, you'll always get what you've always got.

6. **When you mess with forbidden fruit, you get yourself in a jam.** There may be a shortage of eligible men in your relationship demographic, but that is not an excuse to get involved with married men or men who are in a relationship. Some of the saddest people you will ever meet are single women who fall in love or get involved with married men. Remember: There are a few choice words and phrases in the English language that describe a woman who has no morals, but none are more damning than "home wrecker."

7. **Love is a verb, not a noun.** Many women focus too much on whether they are in love with their partner (noun), and not enough effort to love their partner (verb). Love should be an action word. Invest your time in a man who will "live you a sermon" rather

16

than give you a sermon. Action talks and that other stuff walks. Remember: Love is better felt than "telt" (excuse my grammar).

8. **Soul mates are not found, they are created.** Soul mates happen when the foundation of the relationship is built with compassion, consideration, communication, and compatibility. Remember: A soul mate will accept who you are, will bring out the best in you, challenge you, be your best friend, not require you to change, and will bring life to your life.

9. **The last time you changed a male, he was in diapers.** Consider how hard it is to change yourself, so what kind of chance do you have to change a grown man? Men don't want to be changed or controlled. Remember: A man likes to improve himself, but hates being improved by someone else.

10. **Unless the Lord builds your relationship, you labor in vain.** Pray daily that the Lord sends you the partner you need; and ask him for the bad memory to forget the men you never liked, the good fortune to meet ones you do like, and the keen eyesight to tell the difference. Remember: Sorrow looks back, worry looks around, and faith looks up.

THE PLAN

In order to build a house you need a blueprint, to make a movie you need a script, and to start a relationship you need a plan. Many relationships fail because neither partner had a clear strategy or specific goals. Many women go from one failed relationship to another, rarely ever stopping to evaluate what things went wrong, why things went wrong, and how they can do things differently or better. When you fail to analyze past relationships, you oftentimes find yourself repeating the same behaviors and getting stuck in similar bad situations and relationships. After a failed relationship, some women enter the next relationship hoping their luck will improve. Hope is not a strategy. It is a great attitude and mind-set, but it is an awful strategy for romance. Casinos and lotteries are built on hope not healthy relationships.

If you were going to start a business, one of the necessary ingredients for success would be a detailed business plan. The business plan is a document that describes how you intend to operate your business; it outlines your goals, measures performance, and serves as a road map for future activities.

The cornerstone of *The Right Man Business Plan* is the actual plan, a document that will clarify exactly what you have to do to make finding the right life partner and having a healthy relationship a reality. The process asks a sequence of questions that will help you evaluate and examine past relationships, test assumptions, gather and incorporate information about your past and present romantic life, and anticipate the type of social environment you will be working under in the future.

The Right Man Business Plan is about planning; it involves intentionally setting goals and developing an approach to achieving those goals. Here are seven things this book will help you do:

1. **Prove that you are serious about finding a life partner.** Taking time to formalize your relationship

strategy plans in writing, demonstrates you are committed to being successful.

2. **Plot your course and focus your efforts.** Provide a road map from which to operate on your journey to find a permanent partnership. Without a plan, you may shift your short-term strategies constantly without a view to your long-term goal.

3. **Document your marketing plan.** How are you going to find quality candidates? How will you attract them and keep them?

4. **Better understand the competition.** By analyzing what other single women are doing, you'll get a sense of how to position yourself so that you rise above the competitive clutter in a crowded marketplace.

5. **Better understand men.** A thorough understanding and analysis of the male mind-set is essential to an effective plan for finding a compatible companion.

6. **Give you a sense of direction and an action plan.** It will keep you focused and enable you to identify problems early on in your search, so that you will be able to take the appropriate actions to change, alter, or adjust your tactics.

7. **Force you to identify your strengths and weaknesses.** You don't want to start a relationship that is flawed before it gets started. Your goal should be to focus on your strengths and fix any problems that could hamper your relationship quest.

THE COURAGE TO TAKE CHARGE

Not only is wisdom important when it comes to men and relationships, but also having courage is critical. Courage is a prerequisite in almost every human activity, and it is especially needed in relationships. Courage is called upon whenever we confront a difficult, frightening, painful, or disturbing situation. It takes tremendous courage to be transparent, open, and vulnerable with another person. Human relationships are elusive and intricate interactions. They nourish love and joy, and feed pain and sorrow.

Take a no-holds barred, clear-eyed look at your past relationships and evaluate, analyze, and assess what worked, what didn't work, what you learned, where you were at fault, and how you will be better. Be strong enough emotionally to let go of any past relationship hurts and pains, and empower yourself not to let the past dictate your future.

Pay attention to your own feelings and authentic inner voice and give them credence; intuition is your personal feedback mechanism that helps guide and lead you. If you feel he is not the one, he probably is not. Take charge of your own life; and make your own decisions about men, love, and relationships, without being swayed by others' opinions about what they think you should do. When it comes to advice, you always have to consider the source, and remember misery loves company.

Always speak the truth, not just when it is easy or popular. Lies are acts of cowardice. Wrong is wrong, if everybody is doing it; and right is right, if nobody's doing it. Learn how to speak truth to your partner. Be courageous enough to stand up for what you believe in; staying true to your values. You should never compromise who you are and what you stand for to appease someone else. Do not take a seat when you should take a stand.

Continue to learn and grow. You are still under construction; God is not through with you yet. Continue to be receptive to areas in your life you can improve, and become the best you can be. Good, better, best; you shall not rest, until your good is better and your better is best. You must be discerning and courageous enough to be patient. It is not easy to pass on a man who is nice, kind, and into you, when you know in your heart that he isn't the one. Good things come to those who wait. Display the intestinal fortitude it takes to wait on the life partner who is the one for you. Patience is the companion of wisdom.

RELATIONSHIPS TAKE WORK

To benefit from reading and understanding this book, it is critical that you relate to some of the philosophies that are foundational ideas and ideologies for the book.

- **As you get older, it is more difficult to meet a partner with whom you share things in common.** You are getting more set in your ways and becoming less flexible about fitting into another person's world. It is not easy to find a good man, who is not gay, married, or unemployed. You have to be wiser and more discerning when choosing the right partner.

- **Beauty and booty will always attract a man, but they won't keep him.** Men are programmed to respond to certain stimuli, even if it is not good for them; but to keep his interest, you have to be interesting. I once saw a very apropos quote lighting up the billboard of a romantic restaurant. It said, "Looks capture the eyes, but character captures the heart."

- **Men will treat you the way you let them treat you.** Most men will take you for granted if you let them. Do not make a man a priority if he treats you as an option.

- **He is either good or bad for you.** Love should not hurt. He makes you feel either incredible or terrible. He is either a wind in your sail or an anchor on your tail.

- **If your man has fatal flaws, your job is not to fix him; your job is to leave him.** Self-love chooses me over "we." Stop convincing yourself it will work out! Leave him NOW. If you don't love yourself, no man's love will ever be good enough. Men love women who love themselves. Love you some you.

- **Dating is not a relationship.** Do not date a man who is not worthy to be in a relationship with you. Dating is a discovery phase, discovering if he is worthy of you.

- **A good woman should never accept bad behavior from a man.** A man will respect you when he knows there are consequences for his actions; don't let him get away with anything that is abusive or disrespectful. Do not go out with men who have to be told to be nice; go out with nice men. You are worth being nice to.

- **Make a man work on making the relationship work.** The only place success comes before work is the dictionary. Things that are easily attained are lightly esteemed.

- **Abusive men try to make you feel weak so they can feel strong.** Abuse you once, shame on him; abuse you twice, shame on you.

- **A man must leave his past to have a future with you.** You don't want to compete with the ghosts of his past. Try to live in the moment.

- **Women do not attract the wrong men, they accept the wrong men.** You accept a man by what he does, not by what he says. Quality men are out there; you just have to learn how to identify them.

- **You cannot treat a man as if he's going to hurt you, and then expect him to stay.** Do not judge your current partner by what someone else did to you. Let him be judged on his own merits.

- **There is no perfect man, but there is a perfect mate.** Seeking perfection in a man is an exercise in futility; no such animal exists. Seeking a mate, who is perfect for you, is where your efforts and energies should reside. Do not blame a quality man for not being perfect.

- **If you choose the wrong man, you don't have to stay in the relationship.** At any time in the relationship, you can determine that he is not the man for you and end the relationship.

THE JOURNEY BEGIN

Now you know why the book was written, for whom it was written, and the principles that have guided much of the direction. You are poised and positioned to begin to develop the right relationship strategy, to guide you to successfully find, accept, and keep the man you want and who is worthy of you, and can share with you the joy of a loving and lasting relationship.

Reading this book will help you understand why past relationships did not work, and you will learn to make different choices in choosing the right life partner. Never forget or lose sight that the first step on your journey is to be prayerful. What you read in the pages of this book will be helpful; but to be open, willing, and ready for the partner that God has for you is most important.

As a born-again believer, my God is an awesome God. So as you prepare your mental map on how to get to your destination (the right man), go forth and let the Lord guide your way. Here is a prayer that I have prayed many years; it has been a blessing to me, and I know it will be a blessing to you.

"Today I will think as a dynamic servant of God. I am what I think, but I'm not always what I think I am. Clothes do not make the person, thinking makes the person. Therefore, I will keep my thoughts open and active to the voice of God. God did not call me to a life of failure but to a life of success. This being so, I cannot fail, as long as I do his will, allowing him to work in and through me, motivating my every thought. Because my God is a big God, I will think big, with confidence, knowing my thoughts could never be bigger than my God. Today, I will think as the Apostle Paul thought, when he said, "I can do all things through Christ who strengthens me."

As a successful, sassy, single woman, let the Lord guide you on the path to a loving, lasting relationship with the right man.

CHAPTER TWO
QUALITY IS JOB 1

QUALITY SEEKS QUALITY

Thirty years ago, Ford Motor Company used a catchphrase in their advertising campaign, which represented a fresh corporate vision, as it introduced revolutionary new products and incorporated a process improvement system called Total Quality Management, to drive down costs and capture market share. The slogan became a household phrase, it was, "Quality Is Job 1." The intent of Ford was to convince car buyers of its emphasis on quality and to remind workers of quality's importance. Quality is almost becoming a common theme, a generic term that is used so often it begins to lose its meaning. Because it is usually self-proclaimed, most businesses say in their advertising that their product is quality. We just take for granted it is, or else they wouldn't have said it.

What is quality? Quality evokes an assortment of mental images, depending upon your background and experience. How many times have you seen these words: **outstanding** quality, **excellent** quality, **exceptional** quality, **first-class** quality. Because of the ubiquitous use of the word, its true meaning becomes diminished. In this country, we have come to not only expect quality, but also demand it, even when we are unsure as to how it is defined. Quality—like truth, freedom, love, and beauty—is in the eye of the beholder and invites personal interpretation.

In business and in romance, the word quality may mean different things; but they share a common end result, which is to build and sustain relationships. In business, quality needs to answer this question: Did the customer get what was expected for the time or money expended?

Why do businesses try to do the right thing, correctly, on time, every time? The answer: to build and sustain relationships. Why do manufactures seek zero defects and conformance to requirements? The answer: to build and sustain relationships. Why do companies seek to structure features or characteristics of a product that bear on their ability to satisfy stated and implied needs? The answer: to build and sustain relationships. The focus of continuous improvement is, likewise, the building and sustaining of relationships. It would be difficult to find a realistic definition of quality that did not have, implicit within the definition or implied, a focus of building and sustaining relationships.

A business doesn't have a customer until they come back; the first purchase was a transaction. Repeat business is when the customer returns after the sale but the product does not. Repeat business is the most basic measure of quality. Customers vote on the quality of your product or service with their cash, checks, and credit cards.

Having created customer service programs for clients, I know how important it is to listen to the voice of the customer. If you develop a consistent and convenient way for the customer to tell you what they like, what they do not like, what they need, and what they want, you are paving a smooth road to success regardless of what you are selling.

Customers can be puzzling at times because they are not always sure what they want, but they still want you to deliver it. Having dealt with customers for many years, I know for sure that all customers, regardless of the industry or product, desire three things at all times:

1. They want it good.
2. They want it fast.
3. They want it cheap.

Those three things are a universal customer manifesto. When it comes to a customer's desire to have it good, fast, and cheap, they must also realize sometimes "you can't have it all." Therefore, the business needs to identify what's most important in the customer's buying decisions, and they need to satisfy those needs. Why do they do this? The answer: to build and sustain relationships.

For the purpose of this book, the definition of quality is the ongoing process of building and sustaining relationships by assessing, anticipating, and fulfilling stated and implied needs.

THE QUALITY OF ROMANCE

There are three intended results that I want to achieve in writing this book: **1)** help you better understand yourself as a "quality" individual; **2)** help you find a "quality" partner; and **3)** help you have a "quality relationship." Everything I have written is with the sole purpose of achieving these three goals.

As mentioned, it is not always easy to define what quality is, but we do know it is about building and sustaining relationships. Let me explain that quality does not mean perfection. Perfection is maybe or maybe not attainable, but perfection is not necessary to achieve quality. Quality can be achieved by taking your starting point and making it better; not by wishing or hoping, but by doing the actions required to make it better. Are you a quality person? Do you know what a quality relationship is? Do you know what a quality man is?

The fact is, some successful, sassy, single women who did not have a positive father figure, a good relationship with a brother, or positive experience with ex-boyfriends might not know what a "quality" man is, even if she comes across one. Many women confuse what they want in a man with what they need in a man.

Some women will say they want their man to have a big house, a fancy car, and a fat bank account. Do you think material possessions are what make a "quality" man? Many times, you find what you are looking for. Women don't attract the wrong men, they accept the wrong men.

If you are reading this book, there is a high degree of probability that you are not the "average" woman, you are an above-average woman. Because of that, most men will be wrong for you, because they are average. The above-average woman has a higher standard of what a quality man looks like. You can't pull out a crystal ball and predict your relationship future, but you can try to have that future follow the direction you want it to take; and a major factor in following that direction is selecting the partner who is right for you.

I am fully aware that what a quality man means is different for every woman; but there are some universal qualities, traits, and characteristics that are key ingredients to have, in order to be considered a quality person, a quality partner, and to have a quality relationship.

10 Things You Need to Know About a "Quality Man"

- A quality man will only search for, seek, and pursue a quality woman. The movie *Pretty Woman* is Hollywood make-believe; successful men do not marry prostitutes. A quality man will only accept a woman of substance, who has character and integrity.

- A quality man has a set of principles that he will not compromise, and he expects his partner to have principles she will not compromise, not for him or anyone else.

- A quality man wants a woman whom he would be proud to bring home to his mother, gladly introduce to his friends, and envision as the mother of his children.

- A quality man wants to live a fulfilling, productive, uncomplicated life with a woman he loves, respects, likes, and trusts

- A quality man makes you want to be a better woman, and he will challenge you to grow as a person.

- A quality man makes you feel beautiful, inside and out, and provides you with verbal support and encouragement.

- A quality man will give you your space and freedom to have a life of your own, separate from him.

- A quality man will listen actively and pay attention to what you are saying.

- A quality man appreciates attention but does not want a woman who is too clingy and emotionally fragile.

- A quality man wants you to accept him for who he is not for what he has.

10 Things a "Quality Woman" Needs to Know

- A quality man wants a challenge. Do not be so quick to give him love, sex, gifts, or an ego boost; make him earn it. Things that are easily attained are lightly esteemed.

- Do not become too predictable. This too often gives a man a green light to take you for granted

- Always put your needs and desires first, and then decide how you will secondarily meet his.

- If you think highly of yourself in a healthy way and value your time and worth as a woman, he will too.

- Celebrate your partner's accomplishments, and make him feel good about who he is and what he has done.

- Be able to hold intelligent conversations on most current events. A quality man wants a woman who can bring more to the table than a pretty face.

- A quality woman can teach a man more about himself and help him become the man he is capable of being.

- A quality woman makes a man feel good about who he is as a man.

- A quality woman encourages her partner and makes him feel good about his accomplishments.

- A quality woman is classy, sophisticated, knows her self-worth, and is a reliable source of love and support to her partner.

HERE IS A STORY OF A QUALITY MAN

A story: Trish met Vernon when they both served on a jury. It may not have been love at first sight, but there was an instant attraction. At 43 years old, Trish has experienced both the highs and lows of romance; her last relationship of nine months ended when she found her partner texting X-rated messages to some bimbo. Working out of her home as a content editor affords Trish time to be online, but she has sworn off all online dating sights due to her bad experiences. At 45, Vernon is the father of one adult daughter and has been divorced for seven years. Vernon dates a lot, but has not been in a committed relationship for five years. When Vernon asked for Trish's number, she was happy and hesitant at the same time; she had lost confidence in her ability to choose a suitable partner. She decided she would give Vernon a chance; but she would only judge him by his actions, not his words. As the days, weeks, and months passed, it was clear in her mind that this was a man who knew who he was, what he wanted, and what it was going to take to get it. Trish was impressed that he treated her as an equal partner, and he was willing to put as much in the relationship as he was expecting to get out of it.

Trish feels that Vernon truly wants their relationship to grow into something special, and that thought puts a smile in her heart.

The way Vernon treats his daughter lets Trish know that he is a caring man. It's not only how he treats his daughter; but everywhere they go, he treats people kindly, including waitresses, parking attendants, even strangers. The thing Trish feels has separated Vernon from any other partner in her life has been his public displays of affection. He will stop her as they are walking down the street and give her a nice long, passionate kiss. Once when he did it, a cab driver shouted, "Get a room." He is quite candid in his verbal expressions of how he feels about her, making her feel confident that she can trust him and he will be there for her when she needs him. Trish feels safe, secure, and loved, and is willing to give all she has to the relationship. Because Vernon has proved himself to be a man of quality, Trish will risk being hurt and being emotionally vulnerable to, hopefully, take this relationship to the altar.

These 4-Cs are the keys to what you should be looking for in a "Quality Man":

Consciousness. A man who is conscious of who he is, what he stands for, and where he is going; is a man a woman could comfortably follow. He is conscious of the need for an equal partner; he is not looking for someone to be his personal cleaning lady, cook, or concubine. He is conscious that an equal partner does not walk behind him, beneath him, or in front of him, but rather beside him. He is conscious that relationships are give and take, and he is learning how to give more than take.

He is conscious that "like attracts like"; and if he is able and stable financially, professionally, spiritually and emotionally, his chances of attracting a woman who mirrors this are greatly enhanced. He is conscious that before he opens his heart to a woman, he first must open his ears to her and listen to her express her wants and needs. He is conscious that it is not about the two of you being friends first, but being friends always; and he won't stop trying to make you understand and feel that he would be your friend, even if he isn't your man. He is conscious that it is not being together that is critically important, but rather growing together that will keep the relationship fun, fruitful, and fabulous.

Character. Character includes the traits or qualities that form the nature of a man. A man may have power, prestige, and position; but if he does not have character, he will never make you happy. His lack of character will be the major reason why you will get a long visit from the terrible twins (trauma and drama).

Character is the sum of a man's traits, which determine how he will respond in any given situation. A man's reputation is earned on what people see him do. A man's character is what he does when no one is watching him. Charisma and charm in a man may make you want to date him, but his character will determine if you want to be in a relationship with him. You can judge a man's character by the way he treats those who can do nothing for him. Observe how he treats waitresses, retail employees, or his friends. Chances are if he is rude to them that is an indicator of poor character. There is no perfect man; but character is the key factor for determining if a man is perfect for you.

Here are five character traits that a Quality man must have:

1. *Honesty.* A man whose words do not match his actions cannot be trusted; you need someone whose word is his bond and who doesn't misrepresent the facts to make himself look good. A liar will cheat, and a cheater will steal. A dishonest man will steal your joy, your hope, your future.

2. *Dependability.* You have to have a man you can trust and rely on. You need to know he has your back; and if you stumble, he is there to pick you up, brush you off, and put you back on the right path during the good and the bad times.

3. *Loyalty.* Loyalty is the state of being faithful to you and only you in the relationship. A man who is loyal to you will not betray you in words or actions; a loyal man places a high value on the sanctity of the relationship.

4. *Integrity.* This is a man's moral compass, which points him in the direction of doing what is right and doing the right thing. A man without integrity will cheat on you, flirt with friends/family members, and use you to his advantage; a lack of integrity is a fatal flaw.

5. *Respect.* A man must first have respect for himself and want to be a good person and a good partner. A man who respects you will always be considerate of your feelings and display the manners of a gentleman, never putting you in an awkward situation because of his behavior or actions. A man

who does not respect you, personally, and women, in general, can never make you happy or be a worthy partner for a relationship. Watch your thoughts; they become words. Watch your words; they become actions. Watch your actions; they become habits. Watch your habits; they become character. Watch your character; it becomes your destiny.

Caring. A caring man is also compassionate and kind. You should not be involved with a man who has to be told to be nice; you should be involved with a nice man. A caring man will visibly show you how he feels about you through his actions and expressions of gratitude. A caring man has the capacity to forgive and allow mistakes to become learning opportunities that can strengthen the relationship. Most women do not care how much a man knows, until they know how much a man cares. A man, who cares for himself, cares for you, and cares for the relationship, can be counted on to protect you physically and emotionally. You want a partner who is thoughtful and tries to make your life stress-free and fulfilling. A caring man is not afraid to show you his emotions and is not afraid of your confusing his kindness for weakness, because he is comfortable in his manhood. The caring man supports you personally, professionally, and emotionally; he enriches your life, stretches your imagination, and stimulates your desire to be the best you can be.

Caring is an external demonstration of an internal manifestation. You should be able to tell early in the dating process if an individual cares about you, based upon how he talks to you, treats you, and makes you feel. Caring is an action word. It has to be seen, not just rhetorically shared. Make sure your partner is emotionally available and expresses his feelings about himself, you, and the relationship.

Courage. A courageous man takes responsibility for how he thinks, feels, and behaves in the relationship. A man of courage is flexible, generous, faithful, and knowledgeable, without believing he knows it all. You want a man who will assert himself on behalf of the relationship and do the things necessary to hold it together if he feels it is beginning to fall apart. Courage is having the intestinal fortitude to admit mistakes, embrace change, and follow a new course of action. Courage comes from the French root "Coeur," which means heart. A courageous man is not afraid to show you his heart and will demonstrate his affection by hugging, touching, and letting you know you are special to him. His heart reflects a desire to make others feel welcome, safe, and secure. He is confident in himself and isn't afraid to communicate, expressing his joys and concerns, as well as letting you know what he likes about you and what he thinks you could improve upon. This man will make you feel like he is your protector; and in his strong and capable arms, you feel like you can take on whatever the world has to offer. With him at your side, you will always come out victorious.

Many successful and sassy women have fallen into relationships with men who were unsuitable partners. You can be attracted to a man for many reasons: he is smart, handsome, funny, successful, or rich. You accept him into your life because he is caring, courageous, a man of character, who is conscious of his purpose in life and wants to have a committed, monogamous, exclusive relationship with you. This is not about being bitter about poor choices in men. This is about being better, better at choosing a partner wisely and well.

THE BOTTOM LINE IS, BUYER BEWARE

As a successful, sassy, single woman, you have met many diverse men in your life. These men had different approaches, personalities, and points of view. Some of these men were fun, friendly, and frisky; while others were frightening, foolish, and full-of-it. You just read what qualities were needed to be considered a "quality" man. What do you call a man who is the opposite of this? a knucklehead? trouble? or maybe you called him your last boyfriend? For now, we will refer to this man of low character as **"a loser."**

One of the goals of this book is to help you avoid this kind of partner. Not many of you have been immune from coming in contact with "a loser." Some of you were astute and aware of the warning signs and indicators of recognizing one and you stopped talking to them, stopped dating them, or broke off the relationship once his true identity was revealed. The sad reality is, some of you continued your relationship, even after you discovered his loser status.

Romantic relationships with a quality man can be a wonderful thing and what I believe most of you reading this book are seeking; but a relationship with "a loser" can bring you an extended visit from the terrible twins (trauma and drama). "A loser" can turn a happy woman sad, a good woman bad, and a sane woman mad. This poor excuse for a partner can sour you on love, romance, and relationships.

Some of you are loser magnets. No matter where you go, what you do, or what you do differently, these men find you and you accept them into your life.

Losers are dangerous, devious, and deceitful, because they know the language and some of the behaviors of the "quality man"; and they deceive you into thinking that they are men of substance and character. These dysfunctional and toxic human beings are experts at hiding their personality and behavior abnormalities.

Howard Kogan, a director of the Training Institute for Mental Health Practitioners, says, "More people seek treatment now, not because of depression or anxiety or phobias but because of unsatisfying lives, and a large part of that is unsatisfying relationships. There's much more urgency today to be connected in a good way." Some successful, sassy, single women unwittingly choose a loser, repeatedly. The consequences of their choices are painful and emotionally damaging, yet the women that engage in this repetitive and destructive behavior never seem to learn from their experience. Instead, they go from one loser to the next loser, much to the embarrassment and disappointment of family members and friends. Why does this happen?

Later in the book, you will read about the Florence Nightingale syndrome. This malady is when a woman feels it is her job to nurse emotionally wounded men to health and fix those who, for whatever reason, are broken. Many of these types of men could be labeled "a loser." Unfortunately, some of you don't know who or how to gauge when someone is unfixable.

I have not and will not advocate that there is such a thing as a perfect man. I do believe, however, that there is a perfect partner out there waiting for you to find one another. The naked truth is that all men are flawed; and oh yes, Ladies, all women are flawed, too. In relationship economics, the theory of trade-off is accepting the quality a man has, rather than eliminating him for not having the quality you wanted him to have.

He might not be as talkative as you would like, but he is a good listener. Also remember one of the basic principles of relationship economics is, "you can't have it all." Nobody will have everything you want; but in relationship economics, you do not have to have everything in order to have something good. There are some flaws you may have to accept in a partner, but you never have to accept a fatal flaw.

When it comes to the type of man who is "a loser," there are many traits and characteristics that would have him qualify as such. I am going to concentrate on two types of losers: the **mean-spirited** person and the **abusive** person.

BORN TO BE MEAN
A mean-spirited person is someone who is petty, small-minded, ungenerous, unwilling to forgive, and will hurt you intentionally. They have very shallow emotions and connect with others for selfish reasons.

A story: Hazel is a 41-year-old special education teacher, who has been in a relationship with Luther for 18 months. Luther is an AAU coach, who also works for a sports agent. They met at a basketball game in which Hazel's 16-year-old son was playing against Luther's team. After the fifth date, Luther told Hazel he loved her, showered her with attention, and told her he would be great for her and her son, who lived with his dad on the other side of the city. After six months, he moved in with her. Almost instantly, Luther displayed a temper, not always directed at her, but it frightened her. Recently, Luther started blaming his outbursts of anger on things that Hazel did or did not do. He used to appreciate her quick wit and dry humor, but all he did now, it seemed, was constantly correct something she said or did and comment on her weight gain. Luther did not like Hazel's friends

41

and let it be known they were not welcome when he was at home, because he didn't like the way they treated Hazel. She has struggled with his one day sweet and the next day mean personality; it's confusing and hurtful. Hazel told Luther she wanted him out of her place and the relationship was over; but he bombarded her with attention and nice gestures, which made her change her mind.

Hazel's son does not like Luther because he gets no alone time with his mom. Luther will not let her go many places or do many things without him. What is making Hazel consider ending the relationship again is Luther's public shouting match with her in her school parking lot, which was witnessed by a few students. His behavior and attitude has caused Hazel to be paranoid about everything she does or says around him. Luther feels that after 18 months he has paid the cost to be her boss.

Men like Luther will bring you dark days and sleepless nights. Hazel's quality of life is suffering because she has accepted a loser into her life, a mean-spirited loser, who only cares about himself. The Luthers of the world can be considerate and caring, but it's all driven by the motive to control and manipulate you. Mean-spirited losers eventually show their mean spots, and their poisonous spirit manifests itself after a period of time. Give yourself enough time for him to show his true colors.

Here are some of the traps the mean-spirited losers try to catch you with:

- After a short period of time, they will tell you they love you and they want to marry you. They shower you with gifts, attention, and promises. Mean-spirited losers like to move in with you or marry you in less than four weeks or very early in the

42

relationship. Ladies, remember, "If it seems too good to be true, it probably is." Normal, emotionally healthy individuals require a longer process to develop a relationship. Hazel needed more information about Luther before she made the commitment to live with him.

- Mean-spirited people like to put you down. They feel big when they make you feel small. Their intent is to tear down your self-esteem and have you lose confidence; if they are successful at achieving that, it makes it easier for them to treat you badly. Luther was trying to hurt Hazel's feelings by telling her she was overweight and constantly correcting her. Do not allow someone to take something which is not theirs—your pride, self-esteem, and self-worth.

- The losers will try to alienate you from your support, which is made up of friends, family, and/or coworkers. The losers are insecure and think that your supporters might be influencing you with negative opinions about them. Their intent is to isolate you and have you alone, so that their control over you will increase. Luther was trying to come between Hazel and her son, so that her son's negative feelings about him would not affect her.

- The mean-spirited loser will always make it your fault. They will blame you for their failures and frustrations. They believe their temper and anger is triggered by your mistake or your action. The loser will never take personal responsibility for their behavior.

- The mean-spirited loser will not hesitate to embarrass you in front of others. This out-of-control public display of anger is just a mean way to "keep you in your place." Luther embarrassed Hazel at her place of work, without regard for who was watching. This action is typical of an entitlement attitude, which makes them feel they have a logical right to do whatever they desire.

If you begin or continue in a relationship with a mean-spirited loser, you will progressively be exposed to verbal intimidation, temper tantrums, hostile interrogations, and possibly even physical violence. You will be on edge, walking on eggshells, and unable to enjoy life. Ladies, if you are in this situation, I know it's not always easy to just leave or end it; but you must do something before it is too late. Men like this rarely if ever change; they either continue to make you miserable or move on to the next victim.

LOVE SHOULDN'T HURT

An abusive person is anyone who tries to control you physically, psychologically, or emotionally. This person will torment you and try to overpower you through the use of guilt, coercion, manipulation, fear, humiliation, intimidation, and physical abuse. The abuser's arsenal includes verbal abuse, constant criticism, repeated disapproval, and refusal to ever be pleased.

A story: Mina, a 39-year-old front desk clerk at a five-star hotel often comes to work sporting bumps and bruises that she tells coworkers she received from being clumsy and running into things or falling down; but she didn't start having these black-and-blue contusions until she started dating Joshua. Joshua is a

44

47-year-old day trader. Mina met Joshua at a sports bar; they were both cheering for the same soccer team. He was tall, rugged, and handsome in a funny kind of way; she told her friend that he looks like the son that Wesley Snipes and Cecily Tyson would have had.

What started out as a friendship turned into a relationship. Now it has turned into the nightmare on Elm Street, and Joshua is Freddie Krueger minus the long nails. Mina started picking up on some things about him when she would visit her family. He acted as if he resented her doing so; she brushed it off, because he was still attentive. Then he made a great deal of money on one of his trades, and he began to act as if he was better than she was and looked down on her service-oriented job. In his own misguided way, Joshua was invalidating Mina. On one particular occasion, Joshua wanted Mina to attend a dinner with some friends. When she couldn't get off work, he got violently angry; and for the next two weeks, he refused to have sex with her and called her all sorts of mean and hurtful names. One day he was sweet, the next day he was a rude bully. Mina wanted to end the relationship. When they discussed it, Joshua told her she was crazy and blamed her for his behavior. He kept telling her she should not feel the way she does. When Mina mentioned she no longer wanted him to pay her car note, he became violent. For the first time, he grabbed her, shook her, and threw her on the ground.

He felt bad and promised not to do it again; but four times later and counting, Mina is terrified of him and afraid to anger him, so she stays. He said he has anger management issues and he would get help— but nothing. He has not made good on any of his promises. A once fun-loving woman, full of life and a great attitude, has become an unhappy, broken-spirited, defeated woman feeling like she is stuck in her own private hell.

45

Mina shows all of the symptoms of a victim of emotional abuse. Emotional abuse is like mind control or a malicious form of brainwashing. Joshua's methodical mistreatment of Mina has stripped her of her self-confidence, self-esteem, self-concept, and her self-worth. Joshua now has Mina thinking maybe it is her fault that he acts the way he does towards her; maybe because she isn't good enough, pretty enough, or successful enough.

Most of you would never let a person try to convince you that the sky isn't blue, grass isn't green, or that water isn't wet; yet you let someone tell you what to feel or not to feel. Your feelings are your own and they are real. When a person discards your feelings, they are rejecting your reality.

When someone rejects your feelings, it is the equivalent of psychological murder. It's a premeditated attempt to kill your dreams, your passion, and your spirit. Joshua tried to invalidate Mina as a person by telling her what she should and should not feel, by telling her something is wrong with her, and by judging her.

You have to be aware of the different types of emotional abuse and know the signs of abusive individuals.

Here are 10 Types of Emotional Abuse

1. **Verbal assaults** – name calling, with the intent to belittle and berate you

2. **Unpredictable responses** – sudden emotional and irrational outbursts, with the intent to either put you or keep you on edge

3. **Constant chaos** – deliberately starting arguments, with the intent to have the terrible twins (trauma and drama) as constant visitors

4. **Domination** – trying to control every aspect of your life and threatening to end the relationship through emotional blackmail that plays to your fears, values, and guilt, with the intent to have you lose respect for yourself

5. **Denying** – withholding emotional needs, refusing to listen, giving the silent treatment, with the intent to hurt, humiliate, and punish

6. **Aggression** – criticizing, accusing, threatening, ordering, with the intent to have a parent-child pattern of communication

7. **Invalidation** – undermining your perceptions of situations and making you feel that you are too sensitive and blowing things out of proportion, with the intent to minimize your feelings and make you think you are the reason for the dysfunction

8. **Insulting expectations** – putting unreasonable demands on you, expecting you to put everything aside to tend to their needs, with the intent to make you feel that no matter what you do or give it is never enough

9. **Intimidation** – using looks, actions, gestures, smashing things, destroying property, abusing pets, displaying weapons, with the intent to make you afraid

10. **Isolation** – controlling whom you see and talk to, what you read and where you go, limiting outside involvement, using jealousy to justify actions, with the intent to make you feel dependent, guilty, and powerless.

With many of these individuals skilled at making you believe that you are the problem and it's your fault, the relationship is unhealthy. It is critical that you know the warning signs of an abusive person. Women who are given to making decisions out of emotion rather than reason, or need validation from their partner, have a warped relationship between their thoughts and feelings.

Top 10 Signs of an Abusive Person:

1. **Disrespects women.** If your partner does not show respect towards his mother, sisters, or any women in his life, it would be impossible for him to love you or give you what you need emotionally.

2. **Punishes you.** An emotionally abusive person may withhold sex, emotional intimacy, or give you the silent treatment as punishment when he does not get his way.

3. **Has mood swings.** They can go from caring to cruel in 60 seconds— abusive to apologetic in the blink of a black eye.

4. **Manipulates.** An abuser tries to make you think it's your fault that he is abusive, tells others that you are unstable, and wants you to feel sorry for him when he says he can't control his behaviors.

5. **Doesn't keep his word.** An abuser breaks promises, says he cares for you, and then abuses you.

6. **Fits of jealousy.** The abuser becomes jealous over your family, friends, coworkers; tries to isolate you, and accuses you of cheating or flirting with others.

7. **Displays superiority.** An abuser feels that he is always right, has to be in charge or win, talks down to you, to feel better about who he is. Will try to make you feel weak, so he feels powerful.

8. **Controls you.** The abusive person demands your time and must be the center of your attention; becomes angry if he sees signs of independence or growth in you.

9. **Is possessive.** The abuser views you as property, not as an individual; always asks where you've been and with whom, in an accusatory manner.

10. **Will not seek help.** An abusive person rarely thinks anything is wrong with them, so why should they seek help; will not acknowledge any faults or accept blame for damaging the relationship.

Please understand, when I am talking about "a loser," this is not the lovable loser type, who is treated like a loser by others, but who in fact is a nice guy. I am talking about a person who has emotional damage from childhood, which has carried over into adulthood. This is a person who maybe was hurt and has not recovered from a past relationship, and now is hurting others.

I am talking about an angry person, who is emotionally unavailable; an immature control freak, who likes to create victims, due to their addictions and dysfunctions. I am talking about a person with pathological problems that could be deadly. This person may not be in pain, but they are a carrier; and if you keep them in your life, they will infect you with pain and suffering that will debilitate your spirit, paralyze your emotions, and render you unhappy, unfulfilled, and unloved.

When you recognize that your partner is one of them—a loser; your job isn't to stop him from his addictions, free him from his childhood demons, or fix his broken psyche; your job is to LEAVE him. Self-love requires choosing "you" over "him" and protecting your emotional well-being.

How much pain have you carried around while being in a relationship with "a loser"? The costs of being with "a loser" far outweigh the benefits. This kind of person is a liability, which is a hindrance, something that puts you at a disadvantage.

In business, if you make a bad deal, sometimes, rather than just living with it, you are better off cutting your losses and getting out of the deal, even if it might cost you. Once you identify your partner as a card-carrying member of the loser club, cut your losses. Closing the door on your source of pain opens the door to your receiving pleasure.

YOU HAVE TO DO THE <u>DUE</u>

In choosing a business to buy or a partner to be in a relationship with, it is imperative that you inspect what you expect. Everything that glitters isn't gold, so it is up to you to thoroughly investigate what you are buying or with whom you are getting involved. In business, this is called "due diligence."

Due diligence essentially means to make sure that all the facts regarding the company or the person are available and have been independently verified. In other words, it is up to you to make sure you are getting what you think you are paying for.

If you were going to purchase or acquire a company, due diligence would include fully understanding, being aware of, and verifying all the obligations of the company, especially its their financial health.

You would ask to see or know about the following: debts, balance sheets, income statements (last three years), cash flow statements, audit reports, cash flow projections, pending/potential lawsuits, leases, warranties, long-term customer agreements, employment contracts, distribution agreements, compensation agreements, and so forth. Receiving, reviewing, validating, and approving this kind of information and data would give you an accurate accounting of what kind of business or company you were acquiring.

DON'T BE BLINDED BY THE BLING

A story: Deena, a 41-year-old news anchor in a large market was fine, famous, and naive. Married to her career, Deena did not date often and had not been in a serious relationship for years. While emceeing a local charity event, she was introduced to Frank, a tall, handsome, flashy dressing, smooth, middle-aged man. It was evident that there was instant chemistry between them. Deena was excited about the spark she felt from this smooth operator.

In a matter of weeks, after a whirlwind courtship of fancy restaurants, nights out on the town, and weekend trips to exotic places, she allowed Frank to move into her fabulous downtown condominium overlooking the city, drive one of her luxury vehicles, as well as have access to some of her personal financial information. In less than six months, her Prince Charming turned into Prince Harming, and Deena lost her six-figure job, was evicted from the high-rise condo, and saw her personal savings cut in half.

How and why did all of this happen? It happened because she allowed a man into her life that she knew very little about, other than he looked good, talked sweet, and made her feel alive. He turned out to be a thief, a liar, a con man, and an ex-felon, with a history of violence. What appeared to be her dream man turned into Deena's worst nightmare.

Either you know someone, personally, or have heard about someone like Deena—or it has actually happened to you. The wrong partner can have a devastating effect on your life, your livelihood, and your emotional well-being. How does a successful, sassy woman like Deena allow a knucklehead like Frank into her world to tear it apart?

Did Deena attract a man like Frank into her life? No, she accepted a man like Frank into her life, without doing the required due diligence. Love may be blind, but it does not have to be stupid. Before you let a man into your life, spend time with your children, meet your family/friends, know where you live and work, you better make sure you know who he is, what he is, and what he is not.

Your due diligence process should focus on three primary areas: personal information/identity verification, civil court records, and criminal records. Here is a list of the kind of information you need to know about a potential partner before you let him into your life.

Personal Information and Identity Verification

General Records

- Identity verification – important database searches that can prove or disprove identity; discover or confirm "identifiers," like DOB (date of birth), SSN (social security number), and addresses reported on credit applications
- Also Known As (aka's) – discover current and previous addresses
- Other names associated with partner's SSN
- Others associated with partner's SSN
- Names of persons at each address subject has resided; may include spouses, family members, roommates, and live-in lovers
- Phone summary
- Subject's residence, property owners
- Possible properties owned by subject
- Driver's license information
- Driver's record – history and violations; some MVR (motor vehicle records) regulations require permissible purpose

Civil Court Records

- Lawsuits
- Judgments
- Liens
- Bankruptcies – national search by name

Criminal Records

- Federal Criminal Courts Search – all regions, all courts searched

- Sexual Offender Search – State's Databases of Sexual Offenders
- DUIs
- Nationwide Criminal Record Search (DPS/AOC/DOC). This report searches multiple criminal record sources, which include federal fugitive files, department of correction prison parole and release files, national convict database, probation records, and possibly records from other state agencies.
- State search includes subject's entire state of residence; covers a seven-year history; both felony and misdemeanor records, including suspended sentences, dismissals, probation, incarceration records, and those involved in pretrial intervention.
-

Once you have verified his personal history and you still are interested in him, you now ask the following types of questions:

- How would you describe your relationship with your family?
- Who are your role models?
- What was your home life like growing up? Describe it.
- Who are your best friends?
- What kind of social life do you prefer?
- What is your definition of success?
- What does your spiritual life look like?

Successfully utilizing the due diligence process could make the difference between being with a "quality man" or "a loser." Do not leave it to random luck to determine if your partner is authentic and legitimate. If Deena had taken the precautionary measures to verify Frank's identity and background, her life would be different than it currently is. By accepting the wrong person into her life, she now is discouraged, disappointed, and disgusted with herself for being naive, gullible, and trusting.

Many of you will read this and think that what happened to Deena could never happen to you; and I hope you are right. However, for your sake, and for the sake of those who love you, do your due diligence. Do not feel like you are violating a person's personal space. This information is in public records and databases; the only person who may be upset if they found out about your background check would be a person who had something to hide. You owe it to yourself to protect yourself. If you don't, who will?

CHAPTER THREE
RELATIONSHIP STAGES

WHAT IS A HEALTHY RELATIONSHIP?

You will frequently see the interchangeable words healthy or quality to describe a relationship used throughout the book. Recognizing that a healthy or quality relationship can mean different things to different people, I want to define and clarify what healthy/quality relationship means.

A story: Lori and Donny were high school sweethearts, attended the same college, each on an athletic scholarship. Currently, they are engaged to be married, after officially going out together 13 years. At 28, they feel they are ready for the responsibilities of marriage. They have always liked each other from the first day they sat in homeroom together, freshman year in high school. Growing up in the same neighborhood, attending the same church, and liking most of the same things, they were always looked at as the Donny and Marie Osmond of their school. Once they agreed to go steady during sophomore year, they have literally been at each other's side. She attended all his sporting events and he attended hers; they studied together, prayed together, and went on their college visits together. As adults, not much has changed in their feelings and behavior toward one another. Spending time around them, it is crystal clear that they genuinely like and respect each other. Donny is proud of the fact that he has never broken a promise to Lori, which has created a strong level of trust. There was the time Lori was comfortable enough to let Donny know she was uncomfortable about the new secretary at Donny's job, who had eyes for him.

They discussed it, and Donny assured her he only had eyes for her. Their lovemaking was an expression of his love, and he would never risk ruining that special bond. They understand that they spend so much time together that they need time apart. Therefore, they each get a week's vacation alone or with a friend; this has helped keep the relationship fresh.

The outward appearances of Lori and Donny only tell a small part of a relationship story and only the part that they want others to see; but outward appearances are the first signs people see of a healthy partnership. Beyond outward appearances, a healthy relationship is intimate and private.

The 15 characteristics of a healthy relationship can be observed in the example of Lori and Donny:

1. They show a genuine interest in each other and truly like each other.

2. They share most of the same morals, values, and beliefs.

3. They trust and appreciate each other, are genuine and caring towards each other.

4. They are each other's top priority and make each other feel special.

5. They are joyful and calm when they are together; they feel safe and secure.

6. They handle their differences with care, avoiding unhealthy conflict and arguments.

7. Their wants, needs, feelings and emotions are freely expressed and accepted without shame or guilt.

8. They share a mutual desire to protect the health of the relationship.

9. Their responsibilities are a balance between their own needs and the needs of their partner.

10. They know how to compromise but never at the expense of dignity.

11. They trust each other to follow through on promises.

12. They enjoy a mutually satisfying sex life.

13. They take the time to have fun and relax with each other.

14. They communicate effectively with an emphasis on listening.

15. The power is balanced; no one has to fight to get their way.

Compatibility is the trait that I believe is the key to the successful relationship between Lori and Donny. Compatibility is a much deeper concept than just their likes and dislikes. It encompasses eight different dimensions, which are **1) physical, 2) intellectual, 3) emotional, 4) social, 5) practical, 6) sexual, 7) spiritual, and 8) ethical**.

Lori does a few subtle things that keep her and the relationship healthy: she keeps her self-esteem independent of the relationship, she maintains and respects her individuality, she maintains relationships with friends and family, she has activities apart from Donny, she expresses her feelings, and she resolves conflict in a fair manner.

Like Lori and Donny, you can have a satisfying, healthy relationship; but it does not just happen, it takes work. Though they experienced love at first sight, their relationship only becomes a long-term union with commitment and time.

You are on your way to a healthy relationship, if you can find someone whose company you enjoy, someone you want to talk to and share everything with, someone you feel sexual passion towards, and someone you consider your best friend.

A healthy relationship is one in which both people feel a healthy sense of "self." Each person feels harmonious when spending time with the other person. Two emotionally healthy adults try to meet each other's needs, and each can ask for help without fear of criticism.

Below is a list of relationship traits. Circle the ones that are most important to you. Then rate your Top 10, 1 being the most important. If you are in a relationship, let your partner use a different color pen and circle the ones that are important to him. Compare your answers and discuss the importance of each trait to you individually and as a couple.

Acceptance	Gentleness	Responsibility
Admiration	Gratitude	Responsiveness
Appreciation	Honesty	Safety

Balance	Individuality	Security
Caring	Integrity	Sensitivity
Commitment	Liveliness	Sensuality
Common interests	Love	Sex
Communication	Maturity	Shared experiences
Compatibility	Nurturing	Shared values
Compromise	Openness	Sincerity
Fairness	Passion	Stability
Family	Patience	Supportiveness
Flexibility	Playfulness	Tact
Forgiveness	Politeness	Tolerance
Friendship	Practicality	Trust
Fun	Reassurance	Virtue
Generosity	Respect	Warmth

Top 10 Relationship Traits

1) _____
2) _____
3) _____
4) _____
5) _____
6) _____

7) _____

8) _____

9) _____

10) _____

DOES A RELATIONSHIP SCARE YOU?

A story: Ambrosia dated Felipe for three years, she felt so lucky that, at 26 years of age, she had found her soul mate. He was kind, charming, attentive, and so darn handsome. Ambrosia gave him her heart, soul, and body. She was putty in his hands. If he told her the moon was made of green cheese, she would ask him for the crackers. The first year with Felipe was pure bliss; but in the second year, she saw a change in him she would have never anticipated. He became rude and crude right before her eyes; he used profanity, called her ugly names, and even put his hands on her in anger. How could a man so good, turn so bad, so quickly? His verbal abuse had taken its toll on Ambrosia. A once fun-loving and confident woman, she was now an insecure, scared, and unhappy woman. She finally ended the relationship after Felipe brought another woman to his family reunion— with Ambrosia in attendance. A year after the breakup, she is still hurting about the relationship and afraid of exposing herself to that kind of hurt again.

In the early stages of Ambrosia's relationship, she never dreamed that Felipe the man she was in love with would ever be the cause of such pain and anguish. Many successful and sassy women have pleasant memories of the initial stages of their relationship, when everything was nice and sweet, but later something or someone changed and they ended up hurt.

Often a person suffers from relationship phobia, because she is either afraid of rejection or extreme humiliation. Like other women who have been hurt, Ambrosia is afraid of getting into another relationship. You cannot let your fear paralyze you. You need to realize that courage is not the absence of fear; courage is the conquest of fear. Face the fear and, despite the emotional pain, move forward and get back on track to pursue your relationship mission.

Ambrosia can choose to be alone and not date; or she can choose to learn from her experience with Felipe and get back her social life, by adjusting her mental map, revisiting her relationship vision statement and goals, and committing to staying true to her values.

Ambrosia must get in the now and not let the thoughts of her past relationship influence her future. She cannot dwell on what went wrong; it was not her fault that Felipe was a jackass. She cannot let the shortcomings of a flawed man make her a prisoner in a psychological and emotional jail to which she holds the key.

She should focus on the now. She is still a healthy human being, who has the power of choice. Ladies, when you have been hurt, disappointed, and downright lied to by a man; do not judge all other men by what that one man did. Choose to let the next man stand or fall on his own actions and behavior. No man is worth having, if you have to change who you are to keep him.

Remember this about fear: It is **F**alse **E**vidence **A**ppearing **R**eal. There is no failure, only feedback. Failure is about behavior, outcomes, and results. Because Ambrosia did not get the result she wanted out of her relationship, it does not mean she is a failure. Because you choose the wrong partner to be in a relationship with, does not make you a failure. Failure is not a personality characteristic

Here are five fears that some women have to overcome before they can find their right partner and have the relationship they want and deserve:

- **Fear of Rejection.** Many women have been hurt or rejected by a man; and because of that experience, they build a wall around their heart and emotions to ensure they will not experience that pain again. This is when you have to put your entrepreneurial hat on and have the courage to risk love or a relationship again. A failed relationship does not make you a failure. The image you have of yourself should not be dependent on what others think of you. Your self-worth is not tied to what a man thinks of you or if a man is in your life. A relationship or a man does not define who you are as a person or as a woman.

- **Fear of Being Alone.** Too many women are making horrible decisions about whom to date and whom to be in a relationship with, because they are afraid to be alone. Don't be so desperate not to be alone that you let a man into your life that is not worthy to be in a relationship with you. Some men can smell that fear you have of being alone; and they use it to their advantage, by manipulating you or your emotions with threats of leaving and convincing you nobody else would want you.

  If a man tries to play Jedi mind games with you to get his way, you need to tell him. "Don't let the door hit you where the good Lord split you; and get to stepping." Ladies, you can do badly by yourself. You don't need an overgrown, overfed, bald-headed loser in your life. Drop that zero, and start looking for your hero.

- **Fear of Failure.** To overcome this fear, you must act. Action gives you the power to change the circumstances or the situation. Nobody hits a homerun every time up to bat; and yes, maybe you have had too many frogs in your quest to find your prince but you can't quit. Failure is only a problem if you let it defeat you. Failure teaches you what not to do the next time. The only thing worst for you than a bad relationship is not getting into a relationship at all because of fear it may not work out. Ladies here is something I want you to say to yourself and repeat it daily for seven days:

I am not judged by the number of times I fail,
But by the number of times I succeed
And the number of times I succeed
Is in direct proportion to the number of times
I can fail and keep on trying

- **Fear of Commitment.** This is not just a man problem, as many women like to think. Ladies, face it. Some of you cannot commit to a hair color or nail polish, let alone a healthy, lasting relationship. Rarely will you come out and admit that you have a commitment phobia; but you express it in your actions, reactions, and interactions.

You do things like keeping a loser in your life, cheating on a man who wouldn't cheat on you, dating a bunch of men, or not leaving your house to go out with friends, because you like the privacy of playing games with men on Match.com. You rhetorically say you want a healthy, lasting relationship, but deep down inside the thought of giving up your freedom or living with someone frightens you.

- **Fear of Exposure.** Some women put on masks because they don't want to reveal who they really are or what they are really like. Hiding behind the mask prevents anyone from getting to know them. Don't pretend to be something you are not; if a man doesn't accept you for who you are, then he is not the man for you. Everybody deserves to be fully known and to know fully somebody else. By showing who they truly are, some women feel vulnerable and are afraid of being hurt; and they hide behind their mask and keep their emotional distance.

STAGES OF A RELATIONSHIP

Professional, personal, business, and romantic relationships go through predictable stages as they grow and develop. This is especially true for romantic relationships. Having a good understanding of the stages of a romantic relationship will allow you to know where you currently are, what you need to be aware of, and what you need to do. The stages of a romantic relationship are:

1. Attraction
2. Illumination
3. Evaluation
4. Maturation.

As we go through each relationship stage, this is the time for introspection. Take personal inventory and identify what you can do better or differently when it comes to having a loving and lasting relationship.

STAGE ONE – ATTRACTION

A story: Agatha has been dating Esteban for four months, and she has been on cloud nine. This is the first relationship she has had with a considerably older man; she is 27 and he is 35. Her feelings for him are so strong; she believes she is in love. They like the same things enjoy each other's company and are physically attracted. Every free moment Agatha has, she wants to spend with Esteban. In her mind, he is the handsomest, wittiest, caring man on the planet. Every weekend they go to bookstores, garage sales, and rent videos. Esteban collects comic books and baseball cards and has an impressive collection of both, which Agatha thinks is so interesting. Her closest friends are tiring of hearing how great Esteban is. They feel that sometimes when a man looks like he is too good to be true, he just might be. Agatha has had some knockdown, drag-out arguments with past partners, but she and Esteban have not had one disagreement.

When she is around him, she feels woozy or high, and she loves the feeling. Agatha believes that this man is her soul mate, and he makes her feel alive and vibrant. She feels he can meet all of her emotional, spiritual, and physical needs.

The attraction stage is really where most relationships start; it occurs when partners are getting to know each other. All couples experience this phase. This stage can start from Day 1, but it's usually in effect within the first month and can last between three to six months.

This stage could be called the fantasy stage, because your partner appears like your knight in shining armor. You feel like this is the perfect mate for you. You are focusing on your similarities and ignoring differences. You are being driven by emotions and feelings, which allow for intimacy and romance. Agatha and Esteban demonstrate many of the characteristics of partners in this stage. Having an insatiable need to be together; dating is fun and exciting. Everything about the other person is interesting, they have a strong physical attraction, and they don't like being apart from one another.

Agatha and Esteban have never argued: Usually in this stage, conflict is not only avoided but seems like it may never happen at all. Agatha has put Esteban on a pedestal: In the attraction stage, there is a tendency to idealize the other person and have an unrealistic expectation that your partner will satisfy all your needs and wants.

This stage is when your body produces a higher-than-usual amount of endorphins, which is a brain chemical that increases energy, elevates mood, and increases feelings of well-being and sexual desire. To Agatha, everything seems right; nothing seems out of place between her and Esteban. Even if some things would go wrong between these two, they are sure they would work it out.

DOES THE FEELING LAST FOREVER?

Couples in the attraction stage are alive, connected, and at peace with themselves and their partner. These are wonderful feelings and should be celebrated and enjoyed; but the fact is, rarely are they sustainable. So while you are figuring out if your partner is the right person for you, enjoy dating and the relationship experience; have fun.

Go very slowly and don't count on a future together, until you know this man is right for you. If he is really "The One," there is no reason to rush or accelerate the pace, you will have a lifetime together. If you are wrong for each other, you will save yourself much heartache by not rushing in.

This stage creates a heavy tint of rose coloring on the lenses of the glasses that you see the world through; and because of your rose-colored glasses, you may overlook whether your partner is truly compatible with you; and you rush into the depth of the relationship too soon. While you are still experiencing romantic euphoria, here are a few things you **must** do in this stage:

- Do not spend all your time alone with him. See how he acts, reacts, and interacts around others. He may be one way when he is around you and totally different around other people.

- Find out the things you share in common. Chemistry is important, but it is not a substitute for compatibility. When it comes to making two people compatible, it comes down to their likes and dislikes.

- Compatibility is about compensating and compromising as well as understanding each other's strengths and weaknesses. A compatible relationship is indeed rewarding in terms of the physical as well as psychological well-being of the individuals involved in it. What makes two people compatible is their belief in the relationship and the will to make it loving and lasting.

In order to find the right partner, you have to ask the right questions. Some women will ask more questions when buying a new iPhone than when starting a new relationship.

Here are some areas to ask him about:

- Family background? How are his relationships with parents, siblings, and children? (a man that has a poor relationship with family members may not be the one)

- Sexual history? When was last time he has been tested for STDs? (what you don't know can kill you)

- Past relationships and reasons they didn't work? (the best indicator of future performance is past performance)

- What are his thoughts about money, retirement, children, and politics? (is he smart and a deep thinker or just another pretty face?)

- His religious philosophy? (are you equally yoked?)

- Life goals? (does he have ambition or is he a couch potato with a remote?)

- How does he handle conflict or disagreement? (leopards rarely change their spots)

FRIENDS TO THE END

A Story: Tina met Henry at a sports bar, and they hit it off right away. Henry was impressed that Tina knew as much about sports as he did, and he fancied himself as a sports aficionado. Three months later, they are not only in a serious relationship, but they are best friends. Sports may have ignited the fuse, but the things that keep the sparks flying in their relationship is open communication, mutual respect, and the trust they have in each other. At age 34, Tina has been looking for the kind of relationship she has with Henry for years, but never found the man who is almost a mirror reflection. Their friends call Henry the male Tina, and Tina the female Henry. The fact that they were real friends before they became lovers has strengthened their bond. Tina knows that even if Henry stopped being her man, he would always be her friend.

Genuine friendship is the foundation for any relationship; relationships where partners don't give attention to developing their friendship often fail.

In the attraction stage, it is critical that friendship is not taken for granted. With true friendship in their relationship Tina and Henry know that they can count on each other when times are bad; that, alone, generates a considerable degree of peace of mind and a sense of calm for both of them.

Familiarity does not breed contempt; it breeds content. The more Tina and Henry learn about each other in this stage and become familiar with each other's likes, dislikes, idiosyncrasies, and fears the more they become content. When contentment envelops a relationship, it often equates to connectivity, synchronicity, and satisfaction.

Tina and Henry sharing a relationship steeped in respect and friendship makes for a union that could lead to a permanent partnership.

STAGE TWO – ILLUMINATION

Story revisited: Remember our loving couple in an earlier story, Agatha and Esteban, who were in four-month relationship bliss, where they couldn't get enough of each other and hated to spend time apart. Agatha felt he was her Prince Charming; she saw no flaws or faults, and only focused on their similarities. Now six months into the relationship, Agatha has started to notice things about Esteban that she not only doesn't like, but they are driving her crazy. He always has to get the last word in, and he has an unhealthy need to be right—all the time. For months, they never had a disagreement; but for the last two months, it seems all they do is disagree. The most caring man on the planet has become the most annoying man on the planet. She still appreciates his good qualities, but her eyes have been opened, and she sees him in quite a different light.

While the attraction stage could be called fantasy, the illumination stage is called reality. The endorphins, which were being released into your brain at an accelerated pace in the attraction stage, are now being released at normal levels in the illumination stage. This enables you to see your partner's faults and shortcomings.

In the attraction stage, the focus was on similarities. Now that reality has set in and the euphoria has worn off, you can see the differences that exist. Agatha is seeing clearly for the first time in her relationship with Esteban, and she has noticed he has a few chinks in his shining armor, and some are quite alarming.

Feelings of ambivalence toward the other person may emerge in the illumination stage, and you may wonder if your feelings for him are still the same. You want him to change, while yet he remains the same. You may begin to fear you are losing what you once had; and there may be a fear about losing interest in the partner. It is not that Agatha doesn't still have strong feelings for Esteban, because she does; she just doesn't see him in the same light, the light in which he had a halo over his head.

In the illumination stage, romance takes a back seat to reality. You find out— just like Agatha found out— that your mate is a mere mortal with flaws, baggage, insecurities, and bad habits. This is the stage when working on the relationship begins.

In the illumination stage, couples may begin to have more arguments or disagreements like Agatha and Esteban are having. This kind of behavior could make both partners withdraw and feel isolated. If you are not careful, it's in this stage that you may find yourself turning into a person you don't recognize. You never raised your voice before, now you are yelling. You always focused on fixing the problem, now you fix the blame. You willing shared your space, now you protect your turf. You used to be somebody and now you are somebody else.

During the illumination stage, it is important that Agatha addresses Esteban's flaws and any other issues she has with him. How they both handle this potential conflict might determine the couple's relationship future. It is best that they get their major issues out of the way before they can move to another level. The illumination stage typically lasts three to five months.

This is the stage in which partners must have, and use, the following skills: problem solving, listening, negotiating, and conflict resolution. The main goal in the illumination stage is for partners to establish trust, despite the things they have discovered about each other.

Hopefully, Agatha and Esteban's relationship will survive and thrive, because many couples never move beyond this stage.

MANAGING EXPECTATIONS

A story: Fatima recently completed a marathon, which was on her bucket list of things to do before she turns 45; at age 36, she has nine years to complete seven more things on her list. Fatima has always been driven. She is the only child of parents who are both physicians. She has always had high standards and usually ends up exceeding them.

A biochemist herself, she refused to be a medical doctor, because she passes out at the sight of blood. Although her professional career has been successful and fulfilling, her personal life has been a disaster. Attracting men is not Fatima's problem; maintaining a healthy relationship is where she comes up short. She enters relationships thinking they will increase her level of happiness.

The men in her life must prove to her, on a regular basis, that they really love her; and if they do something wrong, she takes it as a sign of betrayal or lack of loyalty. She says she likes strong men, but she has a tendency to get angry when her partner doesn't agree with everything she thinks or wants. In her mind, her man must meet her needs all the time; and if she is unhappy, that means the relationship must be broken. When her parents tell her she has unrealistic expectations concerning men and relationships, she argues that she won't lower her standards or expectations.

Every person has an expectation about his or her relationship with their partner. Some of those expectations will be realized, and some will not. Unrealistically high expectations, like Fatima has, are setting up her relationships to fail. Her partners are being put in an untenable position.

Having unrealistic expectations for your relationship practically guarantees displeasure, discontent, unhappiness, hostility, and the demise of the partnership.

Fatima feels that her partners should treat her the way she wants them to respond. It seems she wants her men to put her on a pedestal; and if they don't, she feels frustrated, angry, and betrayed. Relationships aren't made to be disposable just because you don't get exactly what you want or a partner acts in a way that was displeasing to you.

Fatima's unrealistic expectations and overall assumptions are probably the cause for the demise of what may have been potentially good relationships. Fulfilling and healthy relationships are created, not found; you have to work at building and maintaining them.

Having realistic expectations for others involves realizing that all of us are less than perfect. Instead of looking to others to meet your needs, you must take responsibility for your own life and make necessary changes that are in your best interest. It is important that Fatima accepts her partners for who they are. It is in her best interest not to spend her energy trying to change them to fit an unrealistic idea and image she has created.

Fatima's unrealistic expectations, as well as other women's unrealistic expectations, may have come from her family value or her past relationships/experiences, expecting her partner to provide her personal happiness or telling her partner how she wants him to think and act.

Successful, sassy women shouldn't enter into a relationship expecting to find a perfect person, but rather come in learning to see an imperfect person perfectly.

STAGE THREE – EVALUATION

A story: Jill and Lester met nine months ago at an auction for foreclosed homes. They both buy and fix up houses, and then try to flip them quickly for a nice profit. Since the first meeting, they have gone out, dated, been in a relationship, broken up, and gotten back together again. They have experienced the highs and lows of romance and being in a relationship. They have much in common, but their differences are glaring. Jill is extroverted, loves people, and is grounded in her faith. Lester is reserved, a loner, and at best may be an agnostic. They shared interests, the arts, fine dining, bookstores, travel, and fixing up old houses.

Their six-year age difference occasionally comes into play; Jill, at 36, is up to date with the latest gadgets technology has to offer, while Lester, at 42, is still trying to figure out his Kindle that Jill bought him for Christmas. Jill is analytical, and it is becoming clear to her that she is going to have to decide if Lester is her past or her future; she has mixed feelings due to the present. She loves so many of his qualities, like his warm heart, his caring spirit, and his character; but she is alarmed by his tendency to sulk and be non-communicative. Her biggest fear is the fact that she knows they are unequally yoked spiritually. She doesn't want to let him go; but she doesn't know if it's fair to keep him, especially if she can't see a long-term future with him.

After preparing yourself emotionally for a relationship, you then find a person to whom you are attracted, begin dating, and start a relationship (Stage 1: this stage is considered fantasy). You spend more time with your partner and are illuminated, by identifying and discovering things about them you didn't know (Stage 2: this stage is considered reality). Now you have to evaluate where the relationship is headed (Stage 3: this stage is considered decision time).

In the evaluation stage, you are no longer judging him using boyfriend criteria, but rather using husband criteria. Is this the man you want to be the father of your children, is he the man you want to be the stepfather to your children, is this the man you want to wake up to every morning for the rest of your life?

The evaluation stage forces you to make choices about what you can or cannot live with. In the illumination stage, your eyes were opened to some things you didn't see in the attraction phase; and if you did see them you were blinded by the euphoria and the chemical effects of the endorphins. Now, you have to be honest with yourself and use not only your heart, feelings, and emotions to judge, but also your brain, your intuition, and what you think the Lord would want you to do.

Jill knows that there are differences between her and Lester; and they don't always agree on things, but she does feel connected to him. They have developed a strong sense of trust and mutual respect. The times they have had conflict, they have been able to work through it and move forward.

Jill, like others in the evaluation stage, has to make a difficult decision concerning her relationship; she must determine and weigh her degree of affection for Lester against the characteristics in him she finds hard to accept.

As we saw with Agatha and Esteban, couples sometimes choose to ignore their differences in the attraction stage. They think that as the relationship grows, they will either strongly encourage the partner to change or become immune to their irritating qualities.

The question Jill has to ask herself is, could she be happy with Lester, regardless of his flaws, faults, and annoying ways?

Here are some critical questions you have to ask yourself in the evaluation stage; circle the Y for yes and the N for no.

1. Do you share the same values? Y or N

2. Do you have similar goals about the relationship? Y or N
3. Do you feel emotionally safe with your partner? Y or N

4. Can you express your thoughts and feelings and know you will be heard? Y or N

5. Do you have fun together, and does he make you laugh? Y or N

6. Do you support each other's activities and interests? Y or N

7. Are you still physically attracted to him? Y or N

8. Is there still intimacy in the relationship? Y or N

9. Are you still learning and growing together? Y or N

10. Is he reliable and dependable? Y or N

11. Do you feel loved for who you are? Y or N

12. Does your family believe he is right for you? Y or N

13. Do you consider him a best friend? Y or N

14. Can you see him being the last man you will ever have sex with? Y or N

15. Do you think he is dependable and reliable? Y or N

16. Does he make you feel good about yourself? Y or N

17. Do you feel comfortable sharing your innermost thoughts with him? Y or N

18. Is it comfortable for you to talk to him about sensitive issues? Y or N

19. Do you respect each other's ideas and beliefs? Y or N

20. Do you respect his dreams and ambition? Y or N

If you were able to answer **all** of the questions Yes, then there is <u>no</u> doubt you are ready to go to the next stage with this man as your partner.

If you were able to answer **most** of the questions Yes, then there is <u>some</u> doubt you are ready to go to the next stage with this man as your partner.

If you were able to answer **some** of the questions Yes, then there is <u>serious</u> doubt you are ready to go to the next stage with this man as your partner.

The evaluation stage is where the commitment rubber hits the relationship road.

Not all relationships are worth saving; some have to be dissolved so that people can get on to a new healthier, happier life. The bottom line in the evaluation stage is how you see the relationship in terms of the positive and negative effects it has on your quality of life.

STAGE FOUR – MATURATION

A story: Sybil and Omar recently got engaged. After three years of dating and living together, they have decided they wanted to make it legal and forever. Just last year, Sybil had moved back in with her parents, because of Omar's refusal to give her a ring. When she was gone, Omar realized how much he missed her, and he knew he better put a ring on it or he could possibly lose her. They have learned how to give each other their own space and create a balance between autonomy and union.

By both being 31, they are young enough to want to try new things, but old enough to stick with what has worked for them as a couple—respect, flexibility, and compromise.

When Sybil moved back in with Omar, they made a commitment that they would put the relationship first and make it their priority. The fact that Omar is a personal trainer with numerous female clients has posed a bit of a problem, but they have worked through it. Sybil was able to communicate her concerns and express what she needed from Omar to make her feel secure. They both have set boundaries for the relationship. By doing things to stay connected to one another, they look forward to being married.

The fourth and final stage is maturation. In this stage, you have decided to accept your partner, despite the differences, faults, and flaws they bring to the relationship. You have decided that this is the person with whom you want to make a life. You have both looked each other in the face, and what looked back at you was a reflection of love.

Similar to what Sybil and Omar have done, every person in this stage must take responsibility for their own needs, for their own individual lives, and for providing support for their partner. At this stage, resentments are few. You both have figured out how to handle conflict, and you know exactly what you are getting, with no denial or fantasy involved. Sybil and Omar work together as a team and stay connected, while maintaining their own identities.

This stage would be described as commitment. Sybil and Omar are committed emotionally; they are there for each other, and make the other person first priority in their life. They are also committed to each other's differences, while not always understanding them, but always respecting them. They don't try to change each other, but they are open to suggestions for how to improve and get better. They recognize the importance of monogamy and have verbally agreed to have sexual activity only with each other.

YOU WILL MAKE IT WORK BY WORKING AT IT

In the maturation stage, Sybil and Omar have demonstrated three key things that will help solidify their relationship:

1. Recognizing that they both had busy schedules, they agreed to make their relationship their primary priority and agreed to carve out one-on-one time to make sure they stay connected.

2. They have set boundaries. Omar's job puts him in constant contact with other women. They have agreed that he does not see any of them outside the gym at which he trains them, and he doesn't accept private calls from any of them after normal working hours. They will not allow potential outside distractions or attractions to jeopardize their commitment to the relationship.

3. They have made it mandatory to routinely do things together, like attend church together, jog together three nights a week, go to the movies and have dinner every other Friday night, and visit her parents once a month (75 miles away in a neighboring state). These activities bring them closer and strengthen their commitment to the relationship.

In the maturation stage, the emphasis is on making the relationship healthy. What makes a relationship healthy? The most important part of any healthy relationship between two people is being able to share feelings, joys, and concerns, as well listening to each other in an active way. In healthy relationships, there is no drug or alcohol abuse, there are no affairs, there is no physical, emotional, or mental abuse, and there are no lies between partners. Communication is based on honesty and trust, and your partner is a good friend whom you respect.

In healthy relationships, disagreements still occur, but you stay cool, calm, and collected, so you can listen and hear both the content and intent of what your partner is expressing. You both encourage each other to be their best. You have concern for each other's emotional well-being. Both partners see themselves as equals, no one is the boss, there is no need to beg or plead, no need to dominate or compete. You both support each other's hobbies and interests. You and your partner should have your own friends and interests outside the relationship. As a couple, you can be insulated but don't be isolated.

Partners, who want to work on having a lasting and loving relationship, seek win-win solutions and resolutions when there is conflict or disagreement. When differences come up, try to see the situation from your partner's point of view, and try to work through them.

No issue or problem is more important than the relationship.

Healthy relationships mean accepting your partner as they are and not trying to change them into something you want them to be.

CHAPTER FOUR
MEETING NEEDS

RELATIONSHIP NEEDS, BENEFITS, AND COSTS

In today's competitive, fast-paced world, laser-focused execution and world-class customer service are often the difference between profit and loss. One of the most unforgiving errors in business or romance is not understanding and meeting your customer/partner's needs. This basic, but surprisingly elusive, information is essential to the success of any personal or professional relationship.

I attribute my success as a salesman, and manager, to my ability to understand what customers need and then meet those needs. This talent was honed over the years by doing two things: **1)** actively listening; and **2)** effectively communicating. I have always felt that if you ask the right questions, and listen, your customer will tell you how they want to be sold and what their needs are. Active listening is not only hearing the content but also the intent. Active listening requires comprehending, retaining, and responding. In relationships, I believe a person will tell you what their needs are if you ask the right questions.

Like customers, romantic partners do not always know what they need. By asking questions in a clear, positive, and enthusiastic manner, you can find out three crucial things that will help meet customer needs: **1)** What do they want? **2)** When do they want it? **3)** How do they plan to use it? Once I was able to get those answers, I was on my way to exceeding their expectations.

85

In business, not only was it important to meet customer needs, but also it was important that my needs were met.

In business and romance, there has to be reciprocity and fairness. I had a customer who constantly wanted me to lower my price, or wanted free freight, or deeper discounts. It got to the point where it was no longer profitable for me to do business with them, because I was losing money and not receiving any commission, my needs were not being met, and it was not fair to me.

In business, customers don't always care if your needs are met, as long as their needs are being met; if this continues, eventually the relationship will end. For me to be in a business relationship, I have to make sure there are enough benefits; and those benefits outweigh my cost. If my cost, which was my time and money, was more than the money I was making from the customer, then that would be a failed relationship. If I cannot make a profit, there is no reason to continue the relationship.

The Right Man Business Plan Model is built upon **four Cardinal Principles**:

1. You only date when you are emotionally, spiritually, and mentally prepared to give friendship and receive friendship.

2. You only date men who are worthy to be in a relationship with you.

3. You only get into a relationship when both partners mutually agree to be exclusive, monogamous, and committed, and respect your needs and boundaries.

4. You only will grow the relationship if there is equity, mutual benefits, and minimal costs.

Successful relationships are created by two people who are both whole and have a clearly defined sense of self. This strong sense of self includes knowing what your values are, what you like, don't like, and what your expectations are.

Strategic dating is the key to having a successful relationship. The person you date could be your lifetime mate. It is essential your dating pool is filled with quality candidates.

Far too often, a woman thinks she is in a relationship only to find out she is in it alone, because her partner is still dating other women. You have to have a crucial conversation with your partner, so you both are on the same page, romantically.

Knowing your relationship needs and having strong boundaries indicate where **you** begin and end, and lets your partner know that you are crystal clear about what you stand for, what you stand on, and why you stand out.

A man will treat you the way you let him treat you. You establish very early that you are "Special," and he needs to treat you that way. If you don't feel as if you are being treated like you are special, and you don't say anything; your silence is compliance, and the poor treatment will continue.

Your satisfaction in the relationship will be based on the difference between your benefits (**pleasures**), and your costs (**losses**) of being in the relationship. You need to maximize the benefits and minimize the costs.

Here are five relationship equity scenarios:

1. You are getting **far more** than you feel you deserve.

2. You are getting **somewhat more** than you feel you deserve.

3. You are getting **just what** you feel you deserve.

4. You are getting **less than** you feel you deserve.

5. You are getting **far less** than you feel you deserve.

TAKE HEED OF MY NEEDS

Your personal needs are those things you must have in order to be at your best. Don't confuse a need with a want; a want is a wish, and need is a must. Here is a list of needs, Circle the 10 words/phrases that you believe to be your personal needs.

EMOTIONAL NEEDS

To be told I am loved	Have a sense of belonging	To be accepted as I am
To feel valued and needed	To know that I am a priority	To be desired and desirable
To be respected	To be trusted as a partner	To know that I am special

SPIRITUAL NEEDS

To know my values are supported	My beliefs are respected	Partner is saved

My spiritual needs are respected	My partner loves the Lord	Share my faith
My individual differences are respected	My partner values my faith	We pray together

PHYSICAL NEEDS

To be touched and caressed	Know I am welcomed in partner's space	Tenderness
A satisfying sex life	A partner who expresses affection	Kindness
To be hugged and held	A partner who values intimacy	Warmth

SOCIAL NEEDS

To be acknowledged when apart	Appropriate support in public	To be encouraged
To share fun and joy	To laugh and play together	Hear sweet things
To feel important in his life	To be connected with my partner	To feel cared for

SECURITY NEEDS

To know he will stand by me in tough times	Rally to my aid if needed	Supported
Have input and equal control in the relationship	Always there for me	Loyalty

Know partner is 100% committed	Always has my back	Feel loved

SURVIVAL NEEDS

Risk taking	To know my partner can protect me	Emotional sharing
Financial security	The need to feel stable	A patient partner
Sexual satisfaction	Never to lose my sense of self	Collaboration

List Your 10 Top Needs
(If you did not see anything that represented your needs, list what does.)

1. _____

2. _____

3. _____

4. _____

5. _____

6. _____

7. _____

8. _____

9. _____

10. _____

For each need selected, ask yourself and answer, "Why is this need important to me?"

1. _____

2. _____

3. _____

4. _____

5. _____

6. _____

7. _____

8. _____

9. _____

10. _____

RELATIONSHIP BOUNDARIES

A story: Cassandra is a 44-year-old audiologist, who is in a four-year relationship with Julian. Julian is a 49-year-old ex-felon, who currently is a counselor at a drug rehab facility. The relationship began when Julian was incarcerated in a federal penitentiary; he was the cousin of a friend of Cassandra's. Most of her friends advised her not to get involved with a criminal, but there was something in him she found attractive. For two years, they got to know each other through letters and occasional visits. Upon his release, they agreed he could live with her, and they would see if the relationship could grow. Cassandra is a strong woman with high self-esteem; she let Julian know what would be acceptable and not acceptable concerning his behavior, attitude, and actions. She assured him that she was not afraid of him, of what he had done, or where he had been the last six years. She told him that the rules, guidelines, and boundaries were not to make him feel small, but to give him a real clear picture of her expectations. She said, "I am trusting you with my material possessions as well as my emotional well-being. If you violate either, you will have forfeited my trust, and there will be no second chances and I will ask you to immediately vacate my home." What started out as a relationship "shot in the dark" has turned into a strong partnership. Julian has been a model citizen, a caring counselor, and a great friend and lover to Cassandra. She drew her line in the sand early, and Julian has chosen not to cross it.

To be healthy, every relationship needs space and personal boundaries—both emotional and physical. Boundaries are where you set the expectations for yourself, and for others. It is that emotional and physical distance you maintain between you and another, so that you do not become overly entangled and/or overly dependent.

Cassandra let Julian know what acceptable behavior was and how she expected to be treated. Boundaries are governed largely by how you feel about yourself. If you have a strong sense of who you are and you feel good about yourself, setting boundaries is easy. Because of her strong sense of self, Cassandra had no problems establishing boundaries in her relationship with Julian. If your sense of self-worth is generated by what others think of you, setting and maintaining clear boundaries can be difficult.

The relationship Cassandra has with herself is reflected in the relationship she has with Julian. By respecting herself first, and recognizing her own worth, she knew it was important for her to let Julian know what her needs were and what she expected of him.

Many people feel that they are the victims and, consequently, have no control over how they are treated in a relationship or what is expected of them. They believe that as a partner, their job is to be a doormat. They put the needs and wishes of others before their own, and in doing so, make themselves less independent and more dependent on their partner. When you fail to set boundaries, you are saying everyone else is more important than you, and your needs are way down the list.

Boundaries should be fair:

- Boundaries need to be in the interests of both partners. They should be fair.

- Boundaries need to be appropriate for the purpose. What works in one context may not be suitable for another.

- Boundaries should be consistent. If you keep moving the finish-line, people get confused with the mixed messages, and the boundaries become devalued.

- Set up the boundaries explicitly. Ensure that all parties understand what is expected of them. Set them up early in the relationship, and offer a sound reason for doing so.

- Boundaries should not be about ego and wielding power.

- Boundaries should be set and maintained with respect.

- Be clear what is nonnegotiable and why.

- Offer people choices, with clear consequences if they do not comply. The consequences should be in keeping with the boundary and the impact it will make.

- Boundaries need to be reviewed regularly.

- Model the behaviors you want from others; lead by example.

Part of Cassandra's willingness to set boundaries and hold Julian accountable to follow them was her assertiveness. Being assertive is an act of declaration. Cassandra, by setting her boundaries, declared, "this is what I am, what I think and feel, and what I want."

On her behalf, this was a non-egotistical, active, rather than passive, approach to her relationship with Julian. Cassandra's assertiveness reflected her skill, ingenuity, and energy, to protect her personal space and her sense of identity as well as protect and manage her own environment.

Many people confuse aggressive and assertive. Assertive adopts an **"I Win-You Win"** position. It means being sensitive to not only your feelings, but also the feelings of others, and then exploring those feelings to achieve a deeper understanding of the thoughts and beliefs that caused them. An assertive person uses open, honest, understanding, and caring communication.

Aggressive adopts an **"I Win-You Lose"** position. Being aggressive (or domineering) generally involves having a belief system that puts your values and needs above all others.

In her relationship with Julian, Cassandra did the following:

1. Expressed herself in an emotionally honest way, directly revealing ownership of her feelings and needs, using first-person statements ("I" statements). For example, she stated, "I am trusting you with my material possessions as well as my emotional well-being. If you violate either, you will have forfeited my trust, and there will be no second chances and I will ask you to immediately vacate my home."

2. Did not compromise her own dignity or Julian's integrity.

3. Took Julian's feelings and rights into account.

4. Accepted the reality of her vulnerability and the need to establish boundaries while she and Julian learned more about one another.

When it comes to setting boundaries, being assertive gives you the sense of being "in charge" of your own life, a heightened sense of self-esteem, reduced anxiety, and more fulfilling relationships—whether you get what you want all the time, or not. No one is always assertive, nor would that be appropriate. The question is whether you choose to be assertive when it is appropriate to be so.

List Five Personal Relationship Boundaries

1. _____

_____

2. _____

_____

3. _____

_____

4. _____

_____

5. _____

_____

KNOW WHAT'S IN IT FOR YOU

A story: Kirsten is a 38-year-old professional poker player. Her profession puts her in close contact with a variety of interesting men. She was in a serious relationship with Chip, but it ended when he felt he was not getting out of the relationship what he was putting into it. He had followed her around the country, to watch her play in tournaments and private games. His business was suffering, with his constant travel, and the quality of his relationship with his teenage daughter was also suffering. Kirsten loved Chip but could not let her emotions affect her card playing. Because of his character, she always felt secure and happy with Chip. Dating a quasi-celebrity made Chip feel like he was losing who he was. Kirsten feels bad about the situation because she knows she hurt Chip, but it became clear to her that her career was more important than her love life.

In business and romance, there are costs and benefits. A benefit is anything in the business or the relationship that gives you pleasure, satisfaction, gratification, or reward.

A cost is the sacrifice, loss, or punishment associated with a relationship.

Chip evaluated his relationship with Kirsten and realized he was not getting his needs met. He felt the benefits he was receiving were not equal to the effort and energy he was putting into the relationship.

All relationships have some give and take, although the balance is not always equal. The balance between what you put into the relationship and what you get out usually determines if the relationship is successful.

If Chip had continued the relationship, chances are his losses would have escalated; and because of his failure to receive the expected benefits, he would have become angry and resentful of Kirsten. Kirsten was too wrapped up in her career to be able to keep her eye on Chip's satisfaction level. If she had, she would have noticed how low it was, and maybe she would have put forth more effort to satisfy Chip's needs.

Here are some of the benefits normally associated with relationships:

- Companionship/affection
- Feeling loved and loving another
- Happiness
- Exclusivity
- Self-growth and self-understanding
- Intimacy
- More positive self-esteem, self-respect, and self-confidence
- Feeling secure
- Expertise in relationships
- Learning about the opposite sex
- Social support
- Interaction

Here are some of the costs normally associated with relationships:

- Stress and worry about the relationship
- Lack of freedom to socialize
- Fights
- Loss of identity
- Lack of freedom to date
- Time and effort investment

- Loss of innocence about relationships and love
- Monetary issues
- Increased dependence on partner
- Loss of privacy
- Feeling worse about yourself
- Loss of confidence

List the benefits you want from a relationship:

_____

_____

_____

_____

_____

_____

CHAPTER FIVE
RELATIONSHIP ECONOMICS

ROMANCE PRINCIPLES

In business and in relationships, it is essential that you know and understand the marketplace in which you are participating. To comprehend concepts discussed in this book, it is important that you embrace the following interchangeable terminology:

Business = **Romance**
Customer = **Partner**
Product = **Successful, sassy, single woman (You)**
Competition = **Other women**
Profit = **Quality relationship**
Market = **All eligible partners who would be interested in you**
Marketing = **The process used to find, attract, and retain a partner**
Cash = **Dating**
Cash Flow = **Quality dating partners**
Return on Investment (ROI) = **Benefits received for the time, energy, and effort invested in dating and relationships.**

The purpose of business is to create a customer and make a profit. The purpose of romance is to create a partner and have a quality relationship. Profit is like oxygen for the human body; without profits, neither business nor romance can survive. A quality relationship ensures romance lives, survives, and grows.

How do you create a customer/**partner**? Most businesses are not in the transaction business, they are in the customer business, and you don't have a customer until they do one thing. No, it's not buying something; that's a transaction. You don't have a customer until they come back. Why would someone want to come back, after they visited your place of business one time? Why would someone want to go out with you on a second date? The answer is, because of the experience you created for them.

In business, it was maybe the quality of the product, the uniqueness of the store, the attractive prices, or the great customer service.

In romance, it was maybe the meaningful dialogue, a memorable moment, or your magical personality. Do you know how and what to do to create the kind of experience that would make a potential partner want to come back?

The fact is, in order to create a customer/**partner,** you have to know them, find out their needs, what they like and don't like, and get into their minds and learn how to anticipate their needs. I have always been impressed by the woman who knew when I felt like a quiet night, or when I needed to release the beast, or when I needed a hug.

When you can make the customer/**partner** feel valued, respected, appreciated, and meet or exceed their expectations, they will come back.

Marketing is the key to attracting customers; marketing is everything you do to place your product/**you** in front of potential customers/**partners**. S.H. Simmons, author and humorist, related this anecdote.

*"If a young man tells his date she's intelligent, looks lovely, and is a great conversationalist, he's saying the right things to the right person and that's **marketing**.*

*"If the young man tells his date how handsome, smart, and successful he is, that's **advertising**.*

*If someone else tells the young woman how handsome, smart, and successful her date is, that's **public relations**."*

In business, to make a profit you have to have more revenues than expenses. Revenue is income, usually in the form of cash, which a business receives from the sale of goods or services to customers. An expense is any cost the business incurs to produce the product, such as salaries, rent, utilities, travel, insurance, etc.

In romance, in order to make a profit/**quality relationship,** you have to have more compatibility than conflict. Compatibility is when two people feel a sense of connectivity. Conflict is when two people have too many unhealthy struggles, disagreements, arguments, and destructive debates.

In business, cash is king. Cash is what you literally have in the bank. It is the only true liquid asset; without cash, businesses end up in bankruptcy. The measure of a business's health is cash flow; this is the lifeblood of any business. Cash flow is the movement of cash into and out of the business. When more money is coming in than is going out, you are in a positive cash flow situation, which gives you the opportunity to pay your bills. If more cash is going out than coming in, you are in a negative cash flow situation, and in danger of not being able to pay your bills. The goal of business is to strive for positive cash flow.

In romance, dating is king, In today's society, the way to find true love, have a compatible partner, a quality relationship, or end up at the altar is through dating. Dating is not a relationship but a discovery phase, discovering if this person is worthy to be in a relationship with you. Dating is the first step on the journey to a loving and lasting relationship.

Dating prepares individuals and couples for what they could encounter in long-term relationships and marriage. Unhealthy relationships often display signs as time goes on, and dating allows people to watch out for these signs. For a relationship to work, both people need to find the other interesting and attractive, at the same time. I have often said, "I want a woman I like looking at and listening to, at the same time. Dating allows me the chance to seek out that elusive combination.

The measure of romantic health is finding quality dating partners; this is the lifeblood of successful relationships. Quality dating partners give you the best opportunity to find the right partner. When you date quality individuals who meet your standards and criteria, you are in a positive dating situation, which gives you the best chance to find your life-mate. If you are dating individuals who don't meet your standards and criteria, you are in a negative dating situation, which will make it difficult to find a man best suited for you. A goal of romance is to strive for positive dating situations.

In business, return on investment (ROI) is a performance metric used to evaluate the efficiency of an investment. It's asking a business, what did you get back for the money you spent? This measure of profitability indicates whether a business is using its resources wisely.

Most of the time, ROI is measured by a percent. The higher the percent, the greater the financial benefit. For example, a 25 percent annual ROI means that a $100 investment would return $25 in one year. Thus, after one year, the total investment becomes $125. ROI can be expressed for different time periods—one year, one month, one week, one day.

In romance, ROI equates to the benefits received for the time, energy, and effort invested in dating and relationships. It's asking, what did you get for the time you spent with that partner, was it worth the blood, sweat, and tears you shed putting up with them?

This measure of performance indicates whether or not you are using your time and talents wisely. Most of the time, romantic ROI is measured by happiness, joy, pain, sorrow, anger, anguish, fun, stupidity, and heartache.

If you invested three years in a partner and all you were left with was memories, and most of them were bad, that would be a low ROI. Your return or result was not commensurate with the amount of time you invested in the relationship. If you dated a man for nine months and it resulted in an engagement ring, then that would be a high ROI. Your return or result was excellent for the amount of time you invested in the relationship.

You have to be able to estimate what your ROI will be with a partner, to determine if you should continue dating or staying in the relationship.

RELATIONSHIP ECONOMICS

➤ Economics = **Study of how individuals and groups make decisions to use limited resources.**

➤ Relationship Economics = **Study of how individuals make decisions to use their limited amount of time, effort, energy, capital, and technology to find the right life partner.**

➤ Scarcity = **When people want more of something than is readily available.**

➤ Commodity = **Something useful and valuable.**

➤ Limited Commodity = **Quality partner.**

➤ Supply = **The total amount of single men who are interested in you.**

➤ Demand = **The desire and willingness of single women to pay a price for a partner.**

➤ Price = **Effort and energy put into finding a partner.**

➤ Cost = **The sacrifice and losses associated with finding a partner.**

➤ **Trade-off = Losing one quality or aspect of something in return for gaining another quality or aspect.**

➤ Equity = **Fairness and justice.**

➢ Benefits = **Pleasures, satisfactions, and gratifications a partner enjoys from participating in a relationship.**

➢ Liability = **A hindrance, something that puts you at a disadvantage.**

➢ Outcomes = **The benefits obtained from a relationship minus the costs incurred.**

➢ Inputs = **Each partner's contribution to the relationship, entitling them to benefits or costs.**

We need economics because we, as individuals and as a society, experience scarcity in relationship to our ever-growing needs and wants. Therefore, because of scarcity, people and economies must make decisions about how to allocate resources. Economics aims to study why we make these decisions and how we allocate our resources most efficiently; it is the study of how individuals and groups make decisions to use limited resources. Resources include the time and talent people have available; the land, buildings, equipment, and the knowledge of how to combine them to create useful products and services.

Simply put, economics is the study of how we make choices. Do you get a new car or a new roof? Does the state build a new hospital or a new highway? Economics helps examine trade-offs between various goals and anticipate the outcomes of changes in governmental policies, business practices, or composition of the population. Almost all issues of public and private policy involve economics, and so do your own individual choices.

Relationship economics is the study of how individuals make decisions to use their limited amount of time, effort,

107

energy, capital, and technology to find the right life partner. If you have ever been without a job and began the process of looking for one, you soon realize that looking for a job is a full-time job itself. When you have not been dating or looking to be in a relationship for a while and decide to start again, you soon realize that dating and being in a relationship can be full-time jobs. It takes an extraordinary amount of time and effort to date and actively be in a relationship.

In relationship economics, there are two key concepts that are important to understand and incorporate into your mind-set. The first is **scarcity,** and the second is **equity.**

Scarcity simply means that there is not enough of something to satisfy everyone's desires. Scarcity occurs when people want more of something than is readily available. Relationship economics states that you cannot have everything or everyone you want. Scarcity is the fundamental economic problem of having humans, who have wants and needs, in a world of limited resources.

There is a **scarcity** of qualified men who are interested in you. This scarcity has occurred because all single women are looking for the man who is handsome, kind, considerate, caring, romantic, financially independent, gainfully employed, good with kids, spiritually grounded, and a great lover, who is sensitive and masculine.

This kind of man **(quality)** is what is referred to as a limited commodity. The price of a commodity is determined by supply and demand. The demand for this type of man is high, and the supply is low. This creates a high price. What price are you willing to pay to meet a quality partner? Scarcity encourages competitive behavior. Are you prepared, positioned, and ready to compete for your ideal mate?

Scarcity forces you to make choices, like which of your desires will you satisfy and which will you leave unsatisfied. You want a tall man; but if he is rich and short, what will you do? When it comes to scarcity and choice, there are costs and trade-offs. The cost of any choice is the amount that has to be paid or given up in order to get it.

The critical question a successful, sassy, single lady must answer is, "What price is she willing to pay to find her life-mate, and what will it cost her?" For example: If you gave up the option of dating other men, to be in a relationship, the cost of being in the relationship may be giving up the excitement of dating a variety of other men.

Relationship economics is based on the simple idea that people make choices by comparing the benefits of Option **A** (dating other men) with the benefits of Option **B** (being in a relationship), and choosing the one with the highest benefit.

Price is what you are willing to **give** to get it (effort and energy), but paying a cost is what you are willing to **give up** getting (sacrifice and loss).

Finding a partner and having a loving and lasting relationship is going to require paying a price. Maybe that price is giving up your privacy or freedom, having less time to yourself, showing more compassion, sharing your feelings, becoming vulnerable, risking the chance of getting hurt, listening more than speaking, losing weight, being more patient, being less selfish, etc.

The benefits of choosing a partner sometimes can be fairly obvious (rich, handsome); but they need to be weighed against the costs involved, to see whether rich and handsome is better than the partner who is caring and compassionate. They say experience (benefit) is the best teacher but sometimes the tuition (cost) is too high.

The charge of finding a quality man and having a quality relationship may come with both a high price tag and a steep cost. Maybe that cost is relocating to another city or state and leaving your family, quitting a job you love to follow your partner, or sacrificing the relationship with a parent because they don't approve of your partner.

The cost could be giving up your pet because the place you are moving into with your partner doesn't allow them, or giving up girls-night-out because he doesn't think it's a good idea, etc.

All relationships have a trade-off, which might not be readily apparent or immediately understood. A trade-off is a situation that involves losing one quality or aspect of something in return for gaining another quality or aspect. An example is, you pick a partner who is financially stable but he is emotionally unavailable.

A trade-off implies a decision to be made, with full comprehension of both the upside and downside of a particular choice. Here are some scenarios that would demand a choice to be made:

> You can't have all the advantages of the single life and be married.

- You can't expect to find a quality partner if you aren't dating.
- You can't date losers and expect to find a quality partner.

- You can't start your own business and expect to have a lot of leisure time.

- You can't take a lot of risks and enjoy a sense of safety.

- You can't love someone and not trust them.

- You can't be in a relationship and be free of responsibility.

Romance and relationships is a series of trade-offs. You can have some of many things that you want in a partner or a relationship, especially if you consider having these different aspects over time; but you must make choices. You must lean in a direction when it comes to what you want in a partner or a relationship; and in so doing, realize that "you can't have it all."

If you expect to "have it all" in life or in romance, you will live in a perpetual state of frustration, disappointment, and disillusionment.

Some women will handle this by striving to improve themselves, while endlessly pursuing perfection in a partner or in a relationship that undermines their feelings of satisfaction in what they currently have.

Some women will be locked in a state of paralysis by analysis; in which they can't choose a partner at all, because choosing to have something means choosing to *not* have something else. In either case, what you do have is never felt to be enough.

Fortunately, there is freedom and peace of mind to be found, if you can accept life on life's terms. At any given time in your professional or personal life, you must choose a path. If you accept the relationship reality that life is a series of trade-offs, then you can commit yourself to a particular path or partner without too much grief, resentment, or disappointment.

You can appreciate the satisfactions of the path or partner you have chosen, knowing that **you do not have to have everything in order to have something good.** Moreover, if you choose a path or partner and call them good, you open up possibilities for growth and satisfaction.

This attitude and mind-set brings a mental and emotional relief. By accepting a partner's limitation, you can make do with what you have. I'm not talking about accepting mediocrity or resigning yourself to unhappiness or settling for a loser. No, I'm talking about the deep satisfactions that come when you **recognize the good of what you do have and build upon it**; only then can you appreciate the benefits of the path or partner you have chosen. Then you can be unshackled from the emotional chains of "never enough" and be liberated to the freedom and forward thinking of "good enough."

Relationship economics does not allow you to escape the responsibility of choosing, acting on those choices/decisions, and facing the consequences.

Every decision you make—from whom to date, to whom you choose to be in a relationship with, to whom you marry—will have consequences.

- **Equity** in relationship economics means fairness and justice. There are two sides to the equity coin. On one side of the coin, there is equity in terms of looking at the ratio of inputs to outcomes in the relationship. On the flip side of the coin, there is equity in terms of the traits and characteristics you offer a partner versus what traits and characteristics you are looking for in a partner.

  Inequality and inequities in partners and relationships significantly decrease the chances of being happy and healthy. The more equitable the relationship, the more content and happier the partners are; when the give and take is equal, both partners feel invested.

- **Side one (heads):** A partner will consider they are being treated fairly, if they perceive the ratio of their inputs is equal to their outcomes. Inputs are defined as each partner's contribution to the relationship and are viewed as entitling them to rewards or costs. The inputs a partner contributes to the relationship are either assets (rewards) or liabilities (costs). The reason that there needs to be equity in a relationship, meaning both partners love equally and are in equal control, is that in almost every relationship, one person loves more (ends up most hurt) than the other. The person who cares the least controls the relationship.

113

When partners find themselves participating in inequitable relationships, they become distressed. The more inequitable the relationship, the more distress a partner feels. According to relationship economics, both the person who gets "too much" and the person who gets "too little" feel distressed. The person who gets too much may feel guilt or shame. The person who gets too little may feel angry or humiliated.

- **Side two (tails):** Research shows that most individuals prefer romantic partners who are more desirable than themselves. Many women want certain qualities, traits, and behaviors in a partner that they do not possess themselves. A person's romantic choices should be influenced by realistic matching considerations. This is not to say that one should not strive for the best partner, but in most cases, people end up choosing partners of approximately their own social status.

Relationship economics states that when choosing a partner, there is a compromise between one's desire to capture their dream partner and the realization that people usually settle for what they deserve, meaning similar socioeconomic status and social status.

If you want a partner who has integrity, then you must be an honest person. If you want a partner who is emotionally available, then you must be able to express your own feelings. If you want a partner who has a positive attitude, then you must focus on solutions instead of problems and see the good in people and situations.

Relationships will endure only as long as they are profitable for both partners.

CHAPTER SIX
STRATEGIC DATING

INTIMI-DATING

I am in total agreement with Dr. Phil, when he said, "Dating as you know it is simply one of the most inefficient, nonproductive, haphazard, and hit-and-miss ways to try and achieve one of the most important objectives of your life. It is time to do something different."

To secure a loving, lasting relationship with a person you don't know at all, or just recently met, is a very daunting task. How do two people with different backgrounds, personalities, experiences, points of view, and desires get to know one another? Dating is the answer.

In relationship economics, dating is "**cash.**" This is the lifeblood of romance. Without cash in a business, the business shuts down. Without cash/**dating** in romance, there are no relationships or marriages.

Dating can be both fun and frustrating. To show exactly how frustrating dating can be, a recent survey found women, on average, kiss 22 guys, have 6 one-night stands, and have their hearts broken 5 times before finding the one. By comparison, men, on average, kiss 23 girls, have 10 one-night stands, and have their hearts broken 6 times before finding their true love.

Whether you were married for a long time and divorced, happily married and widowed, reluctantly single, or happily single looking to mingle; the dating scene is not easy to navigate, can be uncomfortable, awkward, and not for the faint of heart.

Many women think dating is a relationship. No, dating is a discovery phase, finding someone to share a relationship. You are discovering if you like this man and want to know more about him. Dating does not have to lead to marriage; but it should lead you to learn more about yourself, learn about men, and learn how to communicate and connect with them.

Something that will help women with dating is understanding the difference between chemistry and compatibility. Chemistry is an intense attraction; sometimes the attraction is more physical than emotional. Now don't get me wrong. I am an advocate for chemistry, because without it, there is probably no second date; but chemistry should not be the leading indicator of why you get into a relationship. Chemistry can be a masking agent, and prevent you from seeing the total person; too much of chemistry is focused south of the waistline.

Compatibility is focused on personality, the things you have in common, shared values, and similar views on relevant areas, such as faith, family, and finances. You can have great chemistry but you can't decide on where to go or what to do.

Your hormones might determine who you date, but your values determine with whom you should have a relationship.

STRATEGIC DATING
Being strategic means planning for success, outthinking the competition, and staying ahead of change. Strategic dating means dating with a purpose, being selective, and a good judge of character. When you start dating you need to be crystal clear on your reasons:

Is it to find love, marriage, friendship, partnership, sex, company, social life, romance, conversation, or someone to accompany you to office functions, so that you don't go alone and look like a loser to your boss and co-workers.

Before you step into the wonderfully wild and wicked world of trying to find a life partner, you need to have a well-defined image of what that partner should be like, act like, and to a certain extent look like. People say dating is like trying to find a needle in a haystack. I say, unless you have a concept of what you are looking for, dating is like trying to find one needle in a stack of needles.

What character traits in a man are important to you? With what kind of personality are you most compatible? What do you deserve in a partner? I say you deserve the best. You have to take responsibility for the people you let into your life and how they treat you.

You don't date every man who shows interest. Ladies, remember, and never lose sight of this fact: You have the privilege and the pleasure of dating a man, but you also have the right to choose not to get in a relationship with him.

Here are some things to know about dating:

- On average, there are 86 single men to every 100 single women. Ladies, you have to rise above the competitive clutter.
- The average man's ideal woman weighs at least 60 pounds less than he does.
- Seventy-six percent of single women date men who are at least 5 years older.
- Most relationships break up after 3 to 5 months.
- Couples usually wait until 6-8 dates before they are willing to enter into an exclusive relationship.

- Most people make a decision regarding a person's attractiveness within 3 seconds of meeting.
- Men know they are falling in love after 3 dates.
- Women know they are falling in love after 14 dates.

BE A CHOOSER

When it comes to dating, your focus and attention should be on what you need and want; and if you see it, go and get it. Women will say, "I am old school," which means they don't make the first move, they don't call a man, they don't ask for a man's number. There's a reason they call it "old" school. Times have changed, and if you aren't comfortable stepping out of your comfort zone, then you will continue to watch Ms. New School leave with the man you had your eye on.

A story: Caryn, a 44-year-old dentist, is currently engaged to Brady, a 38-year-old construction worker. They met at a local watering hole that neither went to very often. Brady was there with a co-worker, and Caryn was alone. She noticed Brady standing at the bar, and she was impressed with his 6'2 frame.

It was apparent that he had been an athlete who still stayed in great shape; but what she was equally attracted to was his laid-back demeanor and the fact that he was not checking out every hard-bodied female in the place. Caryn was never able to make eye contact with him, so she walked up to the bar and asked if she could buy him a drink. Brady's friend started laughing and walked away, Brady was slightly stunned and speechless. Refusing to accept her offer, he insisted on buying her a drink. This icebreaker seemed to work, because they spent the evening in conversation, which led to an exchange of numbers. They began dating, and after a seven-month relationship, they were engaged.

Some of you might say Caryn was too fresh, fast, and brassy bold; but if she had taken your advice, she would still be single looking to mingle. She decided to be the chooser, not the chosen. Some men will be intimidated by this approach and would prefer to be the pursuer, because society has conditioned men to think that way. Some men, me included, admire the courage it takes to make the first move and are flattered by the gesture.

Try it, Ms. Old School, and see what happens. Closed mouths don't get fed; and Old School attitudes won't get you wed. Don't take this to mean you have to be brazen and desperate to be the chooser, it just means you should be proactive and willing to step up your game.

There are three types of women when it comes to dating:

- Type 1 – the women who **watch** it happen
- Type 2 – the women who **make** it happen and
- Type 3 – the women who **wonder** what the heck happened.

Stop wondering what happened to your romantic life. Stop being thirsty for a relationship and drinking the "hater-aide," because women whom you look better than have a fine man and you don't. If you want to get into the dating game, get off the bench, get off the sideline, get from out of the stands, and realize dating is not a spectator sport. In order to win it, you have to get in it.

BEFORE YOU DATE, CHECK OUT YOUR MATE

In business, one of the most important but difficult tasks is to find talented people. The organization that has the best people usually gains the competitive advantage. Part of finding talent is the recruitment interview process. Recruiting quality candidates relies on the recruiters' skill to recruit as well as their knowledge of how to prescreen job applicants. Asking the right prescreening questions assists in streamlining the recruitment process and filters out unsuitable job applicants.

Because dating is essential in finding the right partner, you need to prescreen dating candidates. To minimize dating mistakes, you should know some things about the person with whom you are going on a date. You have to be smart about the men you date. Time is short and you can't waste it on people who aren't a good fit for your life plans.

To prescreen the prospective date, I recommend you talk on the phone before you schedule your first date. If for whatever reason that's not possible, then at least try to chat online or exchange emails or texts.

Here are several questions that will help decide whether he might be an eagle or a turkey:

- Describe your appearance. Can you provide a recent photo?
- What are you looking for in a woman?
- Are you looking for a relationship? If so, what kind?
- What are some things you like to do?
- What would you say are your best qualities?
- How would your ex-girlfriend describe you?
- What do you do for a living?
- What's your idea of a successful first date?
- Who is the person you most admire?
- How soon into the first date would you know if you want a second date?

TREAT A FIRST DATE LIKE A JOB INTERVIEW

A story: Delores, a 52-year-old owner of a floral shop, has been a widow for three years, after being married to Sam for 29 years. Sam passed away after a long bout with emphysema. Delores has not dated since Sam's passing. She does not want to be a perpetual widow but she is horrified of the thought of exposing herself emotionally to someone she doesn't know.

Her cousin Maria has set her up with a blind date, she has literally lost sleep thinking about this encounter with a complete stranger. Her fears come from some of these paralyzing thoughts: what will we talk about, what if he doesn't like me, what if I don't like him, what will I wear? She has turned a blind date into a close encounter of the third kind.

Delores is not alone in her feelings about dating, especially the first date. Even the successful, sassy, sophisticated, single lady about town can be taken aback by some of the aspects of dating, particularly the dreaded first date. Not wanting to appear too clinical or take the pizzazz out of dating, I suggest you treat a first date like a job interview.

A good job interview, like a first date, should be a two-way conversation. The purpose of a job interview and the purpose of a first date are similar. They are for getting to know each other and finding out if there's a good fit. A good fit for the job interview might be skills, experience, and attitude; for a first date, fit might be chemistry, connection, and compatibility.

Whether a job or a date, it's an opportunity for you to market yourself; on the interview. you are letting your future employer see the benefits you could bring to the position and the company; and for your date; its letting them see the benefits you could bring to their life.

The job interview gives you an opportunity to discover if you want to work for the company; and the first date gives you the opportunity to see if you would be interested in wanting to get to know this man more; and if you would want a second date.

A job interview and a first date are visual inspections. First impressions are nearly impossible to reverse; so with both the interview and the first date, you should be dressed appropriately and conduct yourself in a professional and respectful manner. The image you present communicates what you think of yourself and what you think of the interviewer—or your date.

Treating a first date like a job interview doesn't mean you have to make your date feel like he's being interrogated or taking a "do you want to be my husband exam." It just means be relaxed, conversational, and charming.

During the interview, the employer will be assessing you in the following areas:

1. Your ability to do the job – Can you apply your education, experience, and training, to their workplace?
2. Your work ethic – What motivates you to take initiative and work hard; how have you demonstrated leadership capabilities?
3. Your ability to "fit" with their organization – How well do you work with others as a team?

During the first date, the man will be assessing you in the following areas:

1. Your ability to hold a conversation – Are you intelligent, articulate, with a sense of humor?

2. Your personality – Are you fun, funny, kind, witty, extroverted/introverted, stuck up?
3. Your appearance – Are you pretty, sexy, is there some body heat between you two, do you get his motor running?

A story: Lauren is a receptionist at a large law firm. She wanted to be a lawyer after getting her degree in political science, but never scored high enough on the LSAT to be accepted into a law school. Her hopes now are to become a law clerk; she took her current role to get her foot in the door at the firm. She recently was asked out on a date by Thomas, a courier who delivers documents to the office. She accepted, although she didn't know him very well. They met at a family-owned restaurant, which was quiet and quaint. Thomas made her slightly uncomfortable, because he was quiet and somewhat reserved, but it was only after she found out that *The Godfather* was his favorite movie did the evening pick up.

Lauren saw the spark in his eye, when she mentioned it was her favorite movie also. The rest of the night was a *Godfather* trivial pursuit game. Thomas was beaming when she couldn't answer the question, "Name the head of the five families that Michael Corleone killed." Then he recited them as Lauren looked in amazement. She was able to see a side of him that was enjoyable and fun and made her feel closer to him. As they were leaving the restaurant, he thanked her for one of the best dates he had ever had and asked if she go out with him again.

The deciding factor for the interviewer to bring you back for the second round of interviews, or the date to ask you out again, is how you made them feel. Did they feel good about you, and did you make them feel good about themselves?

The best way to get someone to feel good about you is by being interested in them and the things in which they have an interest. Lauren had a good first date, because she was able to find the spark that ignited Thomas to open up and be himself.

The royal road to a person's heart is to find out the things they treasure, and then let them talk and share those things.

DATING SHOULD BE FUN

If you are so worried about going on a date, it will be difficult for you to relax and enjoy the experience. You should not put pressure on yourself to have to be perfect or expect the date to lead to the altar. If you worry so much about whether your date will like you, there is no way you can be at your best, and your date may not get a chance to see the real you.

The idea of dating is to see if you feel a mutual and natural attraction. Dating is not life or death. Enjoy it for what it is— meeting, socializing, and spending time with a person who hopefully is interesting, but may not play any significant role in your life. Lauren was able to have fun and a pleasant evening, because she was relaxed and had no expectations other than to make it a good date.

What makes a date an enjoyable experience? If a date doesn't end up in a meaningful relationship, was it a failure? Meeting new people and maybe becoming just friends is justification for taking the time to go out on a date. To help ensure the date will be good, you should choose a public place, a pleasant activity you both would enjoy, but not where it's so loud you have no time for a private conversation.

Be positive that it will go well; but have an escape plan if it isn't going great, and a plan to extend the date. if it is going extremely well. A good date is really about having a fun experience, where you enjoyed yourself, even if it was not a love connection.

DATING <u>DO'S</u> AND <u>DON'TS</u>

If dating is a game, then just like any other game, there are rules you need to study, learn, and follow. Knowing the rules in any game gives you an opportunity to play on a level field. You can separate rules into two parts: Do's and Don'ts. Both areas have distinct guidelines that a successful, sassy woman should follow for dating success.

DATING <u>DO'S</u>

- **Do** look your best. The first things he will notice about you are your looks. You never get a second chance to make a first impression. Have your hair and hands looking great. Treat each date as if he may be "The One."

- **Do** make the best out of the date; enjoy yourself, have fun, relax and smile.

- **Do** compliment him on how he looks, or find something nice to say about him. It's nice to hear and puts him in a good frame of mind.

- **Do** be punctual; showing up late is not as fashionable as it once was.

- **Do** listen to him, be interested and interesting. Ask good questions and listen to what he says he likes to read, watch, and participate in. Make good eye contact.

- **Do** let him pay; you can learn a lot about him by how he handles the financial aspects of the date.

- **Do** pay attention to him. One way to get a man's attention on a date is to pay a lot of attention to him. Rather than talking about yourself, ask him a lot of questions.

- **Do** be warm, friendly, and happy; hopefully, you will get the same in return.

- **Do** call or e-mail the day after, to thank them for a nice time, even if you don't want a second date.

- **Do** turn off your Blackberry or cell phone; leaving it on to ring incessantly is rude.

- **Do** Google him before you go out on a first date. Always better to be safe than sorry.

DATING DON'TS

- **Don't** be dishonest about aspects of your life. Honesty is always the best policy, even if it may not be so flattering. A lie, on a date, could prevent having a relationship in the future.

128

- **Don't** be so revealing about your personal life, in the beginning. Getting to know someone takes time; sharing inner secrets early could come back to hurt you later.

- **Don't** give out personal information on a first date, like your phone number or address. Keep this information private until you believe he is trustworthy.

- **Don't** date people who are bad for you. You know the type who has hurt you in the past. Break the pattern of being attracted to the wrong kind of man.

- **Don't** be rude or too risqué on a date. How you act early is how you will be treated later. Don't tell dirty, political, or religious jokes until after you get to know one another.

- **Don't** be naïve by ignoring your personal safety; carry your cell phone, tell a friend where you are going and when you will be back (on the first date). Don't go anywhere or do anything that doesn't fit into your comfort zone. If you want to have a glass of wine or cocktail, invoke the no more than two drinks rule.

- **Don't** talk about old boyfriends and past relationships.

- **Don't** look at other men when you are on a date. Keep your attention on him.

- **Don't** tolerate being disrespected or treated badly, excuse yourself and head for the nearest exit if you feel threatened or uncomfortable. A good woman should never accept bad behavior.

- **Don't** date a married man—**ever**. Some of the most miserable, unhappy, and angry women are those who date married men; find someone who is emotionally and legally available. Date a married man, and you are inviting the terrible twins (trauma and drama) to live with you.

(None of these Do's and Don'ts is set in stone, and there are exceptions to every rule, but they are good guidelines to follow).

ONLINE DATING – HIGH TECH/LOW TOUCH-

A story: Alexis, the 46-year-old senior manager at a major retail chain, is a self-proclaimed workaholic. She is at work by 6:00 a.m. and normally leaves at 8:00 p.m.; her schedule makes it difficult to have much of a social life. She believes being in retail and her desire to climb the corporate ladder was responsible for ruining her marriage. Her ex-husband was a police officer, who wanted a more traditional wife and a less hectic life; he used to tell her that nobody on their death bed ever said I wish I had spent more time at the office. Alexis knows she isn't going to change her work lifestyle, but she does miss the intimacy of being in a relationship. Her friends have encouraged her to go on an online dating site to find a partner.

Alexis used to think online dating was for the unattractive, homely woman who couldn't get a date in the real world; but now she has changed her thinking, because of the many success stories about online dating. Feeling somewhat desperate about her lack of dating options, Alexis has considered going out with someone who is not in her league.

Alexis, like other women, has spent more time at the office than she probably should have. All work and no play make her not very date-able. She is considering dating online but feels uncomfortable; she is feeling desperate, so she is thinking about lowering her standards and dating someone who is not in her league. STOP. Desperate women do desperate things, like don't care who the guy is or what he does as long as she's not alone. Ladies, this is a recipe for disaster. If you feel you are nearing the desperate zone, you need to call a timeout and get a checkup from the neck-up. Speaking of checkup; you need to see if you have any of the 10 signs and symptoms of a desperate woman.

You may be a desperate woman, if you are doing some of the following:

- **Getting deeply involved after a few dates.** This is a major red flag; it reeks of needy and clingy, and most quality men are allergic to that, I know I am.

- **Excessive communication.** The need to constantly call, text, tweet, e-mail, or carrier pigeon makes you look insecure and makes him look for company elsewhere.

- **Wanting to be friends with his friends.** Attaching yourself to his social circle without an invitation makes you look like you have no friends of your own, which makes him think there must be a reason you have no friends.

- **Spending all your free time with him.** Men like some personal time and space; when you invade theirs and never want to leave, it makes you seem like you don't have a life of your own.

- **Buying things for him.** Once or twice is cute and kind; much more than that is annoying. It looks like you are trying to buy his affection.

- **Trying too hard.** Dressing too sexy or overeager to please, is trying too hard. Men like sweet but not to excess.

- **Pressuring to meet his family.** Relationships grow on their own; when you try to force it, you may force him to move on.

- **Dating losers.** Times may be tough in the dating world; but if you know you are in the 8-10 range, and you are going out with men in the 3-5 range, time to take a dating vacation and wait while you get your mojo back.

- **Always being agreeable.** All his jokes aren't funny, all his viewpoints aren't correct, and it's okay not to laugh or you can even tell him he's all wet. No man likes a pushover, for very long.

- **Hate being alone.** Constantly asking him to come over or asking can you come over makes most men think you may have an attachment issue, which usually makes him detach.

If you see any of yourself in any of these examples, you may want to call an intervention and have your friends scare you straight and help you regain your confidence.

YOU LOOK LIKE WHO?

Many professional women like Alexis are too busy to date. These successful, sassy, single women don't have the time and, in many cases, the emotional energy to mix, mingle, and meet new people. The answer for Alexis is to start dating on the internet. Forty million Americans use an online dating service; that is about 40 percent of the American single population.

The personal computer is the 21st Century's No. 1 matchmaker.

Having had personal experience with online dating, I can honestly say that the internet is a good way to meet people. I have had positive encounters and some not so positive. After being persuaded by a friend that I wouldn't be officially declared a loser by going on the internet, I signed up to give it a try. My first encounter was not a positive one. I was afraid to put my picture on the site, and I was too green to ask to see a potential date's photo. I was contacted by a woman with no picture on the site, but who lived in my city. We shared a series of e-mails and then progressed to phone conversations.

During a conversation I asked her whom did people say that she looked like; and without hesitation, she responded, the movie star Vivica Fox. I was more comfortable, believing that she had to be pretty, curvy, and sexy. With my newfound confidence, we agreed to meet for dinner, after I returned from a business trip. Upon my return, I was filled with that excitement you get when you go on a first date.

It was terrible weather that night—snow, cold and ice; but being a trooper, I headed out to meet the lady who could possibly be "the one." I arrived early at this trendy and expensive restaurant; I positioned myself at the bar, so I could see the door and all who entered. My mind and eyes were focused on a tall, good-looking, foxy lady, when a woman walks up to me and says, "Are you Ron?" I was shocked, wondering how this stranger could guess my name. Maybe this was my date's sister telling me her sister was sick and couldn't make it. Then she said her name and I almost fell out of my chair. This woman was my date.

Now I was in an ethical crisis. I could lie and say my name was Oscar and leave; I could say, "Yes I am Ron," then excuse myself, go to the restroom, and crawl out of the window; or I could man-up and say, "Hello, it's a pleasure to finally meet you, up close and personal" (which is what I chose to do). Standing in front of me was not a replica of Vivica Fox but the spitting image of Nell Carter, another actress who was as wide as she was tall.

After my shock wore off, and we sat down to dinner, I found out my date was a smart and funny lady. I was tempted the whole night to ask her why she thought people felt she looked like Vivica Fox, but being the gentlemen I am, I didn't. She invited me to her house for a second date, which I accepted. She cooked one of the best steaks I ever had. She became a friend, but I was not interested in any benefits. That was a learning experience, and I never met anyone again without seeing their picture first.

For Alexis, and women like her, an online dating relationship can be appealing. You don't have to show yourself to someone in whom you may not be interested. Instead of rushing to meet, you can get to know them by e-mail, private chatting online, or the phone. You can get comfortable with a person before you decide to meet.

Sometimes this comfort results in the unfortunate reality that too many first dates are highly sexual. A survey, conducted by the Singles in America organization, found that 55 percent of singles reported having had sex on the first date (66 percent of men, 44 percent of women). What, in the past, would be considered a first date (meaning this is the first time you have actually seen each other in person), doesn't feel that way anymore for many women. Because of online dating and social media, there has already been flirting and sexual tension. This makes the first physical date feel like the third or fourth date. The survey also found that 21 percent of singles met the last person they dated online, which is the most often cited way of meeting.

There are some precautions that need to be taken, if you are going to date online.

EIGHT THINGS YOU NEED TO BE AWARE OF WITH ONLINE DATING

- Men will **misrepresent** who and what they are. It is easy to falsify a profile or a picture. Don't fall hook, line, and sinker for what a person says over the internet. As a rule of thumb, when a man describes himself, subtract three inches from his height, add 25 pounds to his weight, halve his income, and add a decade to his age.

- Don't share any personal information that could lead someone to find your address, home phone, last name, or an e-mail address that includes your name.

- Don't invest too much time e-mailing one another, move from e-mail to cell phone sooner rather than later. In a phone chat, you'll get a better sense of whether your personalities click and if you feel a connection. Sometimes a voice can turn you off or turn you on. Mike Tyson or Barry White, which voice would you choose?

- Always represent yourself accurately; be truthful about your weight, height and age. If you meet; he will obviously find out you weren't honest and may not trust anything else you might say.

- Spell it out very clearly that you don't and won't date married men. Married men are using the internet to cheat or establish friends with benefits arrangements.

- If you agree to meet someone, meet him in a public place for the first few dates. Don't invite him into your home, regardless of what lame excuse he may use.

- Online dating can be a nice way to pass the time, but don't get trapped into the see how many men you can talk to syndrome. There is no shortage of available men online. Don't let the internet turn you from a rake to a hoe.

- If someone is annoying you or harassing you, block them instantly. Some guys on the internet have issues, and you don't want to be on the other end of his psychosis. Trust your intuition; if he talks like a nut and acts like a nut, he is a nut.

IS A HOOK-UP A DATE?

A story: Juanita, a 26-year-old graduate school student believes that being in a relationship would take away from her studies and be a distraction. Dating to her is old-fashioned and is what her parents did. She believes dating leads to relationships, relationships lead to marriage, and she isn't interested in either. She does have her hook-ups, which are interactions that sometimes include casual sex. She doesn't want to invest any emotional energy to release her sexual energy. Many of her friends are proponents of the hook-up and don't feel it is demeaning to have meaningless carnal knowledge. Juanita feels empowered and in total control of her social life, and she has no guilt about her multiple hook-ups.

Hooking up is what many people, especially younger people, would define as having intercourse with a zero-to-sex pick-up speed; it could be within hours of meeting, after some light conversation, or after a couple shots of Patron. Hooking up is such a vague term. We really don't know if it means the man got to first base, second base, third base, or if he scored.(something tells me, he scores.)

Juanita has no time for a relationship that might require a commitment. Dating doesn't fit into her priorities. She has too many things to do and not enough time to date; so she just hooks-up with someone, which in her mind is a spontaneous sexual encounter with no strings attached.

While Juanita might be collecting more sexual notches in her Michael Kors belt, she is devaluing what is a most precious gift.

Hooking-up is the modern-day version of a booty-call or a one-night stand. This lifestyle has a high risk and low reward factor. Hook-ups rarely, if ever, result in a healthy and lasting relationship.

SLOW DOWN

A story: Rena met Todd through a mutual friend. Todd is 29, 5 years older than Rena, who thinks the age difference is mysteriously sexy. They both are personal trainers and share the belief that a healthy body helps to keep a healthy mind. They have gone out twice, and both times were better than expected. Rena has a light complexion, and Todd is jet black. The contrast in hues is a big turn-on for Rena. Todd made it clear, after the second date that he would love to experience Rena from head to toe and everywhere in between. The thought of being with Todd intimately is intoxicating to Rena; but she is torn, she really doesn't know him that well, and what would he think of her if she gave up the goodies so early.

Then the little devil with the pitchfork on her shoulder whispers, "if you don't give it up, he will drop you like a bad habit." This dilemma is confusing her and making her doubt her decision making mechanism.

When you begin a new job, you are normally put on what they call a probationary period. This probationary period exists to help ensure that, as a new employee, you are making adequate progress in learning your new position. During this period, you and your supervisor should have close contact, in order to promote a strong working relationship.

A number of formal evaluations are made to assess your ability to do the job. During this period, you are **not** entitled to the benefits that a full-time employee would receive. If you choose not to wait until you are married to have sexual relationships, I recommend you adapt your own personal probationary period before you engage in sex; especially if you are truly looking to find your life partner. My feeling has been that when two people see each other naked, it changes the dynamic of the relationship. Expectations change, and feelings and emotions come more into play.

Sex often clouds a woman's mind, and cloudy minds contribute to bad decisions and irrational behaviors. This waiting time gives you an opportunity to determine if this man is dependable, and if he has adjusted, adapted, and understood your emotional needs. When you eliminate sex from the dating equation, it gives you more of an accurate snapshot of what you and this man have in common.

Truth be told, most "quality" men who are looking for a serious relationship, respect and admire a woman's sexual restraint. There is no magic number of days that will assure you the time is right; only you can determine that time. Maybe that time is marriage (interesting thought).

VALUE YOUR GIFT

After listening to, reading about, and researching romance, intimacy, and relationships, I have concluded women (collectively) have lost a sense of value for their sexuality and the gift of lovemaking. A woman's body should be respected, cherished, valued, and shared with very few deserving people. As soon as you start sharing the gift with anyone and without care, the gift starts to lose value. The more people use the gift, the more it depreciates and the less appeal it has.

Juanita looks at sex as fun and pleasurable; but in the process, she has forgotten that it is a gift which quality men value. If she doesn't value her gift, why should anyone else? Most men wouldn't want a gift that many others have received. Some successful, sassy women are mistaking sex for love. Because you have sex with a man doesn't mean you are in a relationship. Men have a tendency to place women in two categories: Ms. Right and Ms. Right Now. The way he chooses to put you in a category is by what you say and do around him. Sleep with him too soon and you could end up in the Ms. Right Now category.

Show him you value your gift. If he wants to share it, he is going to have to prove to you that he has what it takes to be in a serious relationship. No matter how much a man thinks he might be the bomb.com, he still thinks in the back of his mind that if you slept with him early in the relationship, you have done it before and probably will do it again.

Ladies, the Word says your body is a temple of the Holy Spirit. Once you realize the truth and accept that mantra, certain things will happen: 1) you will treat your body as a treasure and respect the gift; 2) you will realize that a good man will be patient and wait until you are ready to share the gift with him; and 3) when you are sure the time is right for the gift to be shared, the passion will be multiplied.

DATING HEALTHY

It is very difficult to have a healthy relationship, if you aren't dating in a healthy way. A critical component of healthy dating is that you must be able to be yourself. It is important that you don't feel the need to change to be appreciated or accepted. You should also accept your partner for who he is.

People can change, but you can't change them. If you are not suitable to this person the way you are right now, then **don't** continue dating them, because it will probably not lead to having a relationship. Dating is your means to find or be found by a potential life partner; it's also the time to find out if he is or isn't the one.

Healthy dating demonstrates mutual respect, trust, and honest communication. Your partner must respect your personal space, your time, and your relationships with other people. Healthy dating would never make you feel pressured to do something that you don't want to do; dating decisions are made on values not fear, guilt, or need.

Healthy relationships must have emotional and physical boundaries; boundaries describe what you are and what you are not, what you will and will not tolerate. Boundaries keep good things in and bad things out. Dating boundaries are like a fence that is protecting your emotional property (heart and feelings). In a healthy relationship, each partner respects the other's boundaries. Thoughts regarding physical intimacy need to be discussed early on in healthy relationships, to properly manage expectations.

Your boundaries are nonnegotiable standards of performance. These are things you must do or not do and are not open for debate or discussion. When a man dates you, he is basically saying, "I want to get to know you." What this really means is that he wants to see what he can get and what you are willing to give. Now, this gives you the opportunity to set some standards of behavior or restrictions that are nonnegotiable, and this will let him know very clearly what you are about and what you are **not** about.

EXAMPLES OF NONNEGOTIABLE STANDARDS OF PERFORMANCE:

- Under no circumstances will you date a man who is married, living with someone, or in a relationship. Some deceitful men will try to make you believe that they are single. If a man lies, he may cheat; if he cheats, he may steal; if he steals, he may kill. Don't let a man's lie cheat you of having an honest relationship, by stealing your peace of mind and killing your romantic dreams.

- Don't be with someone who doesn't want to be with you. If his actions show he isn't that into you, cut your losses early and move on. A man's actions, not his words, really tell you what he thinks of you.

- You will not tolerate or accept being disrespected by his words, deeds, body language, attitudes, or his apathetic ways. A man will treat you the way you let him treat you; it's important that you not accept any less than his best.

- You will have a balanced relationship; everything cannot and will not be dictated by him or be done on his terms. Once you establish that you don't dance to

142

his music, and you have an opinion and a voice and you will be heard, it will set a tone for how dating goes.

- If you break one of society's boundaries (the law), there is a consequence (you get arrested). I have played sports at every level—high school, college, and professionally—and I learned that if you don't play within the boundaries (rules), you get penalized. Your partner must understand that if they don't stay within your dating boundaries, there will be a penalty to pay; and it could be that they lose the pleasure and privilege of your time and interest.

Healthy dating is the gateway to a healthy relationship, and knowing the signs is important.

LOOK FOR THE EVIDENCE

A story: Freda and Al have been dating for three months. They met at a political debate; interestingly enough, Freda is a Democrat, and Al is a Republican. On the first date, Al listened to Freda's viewpoints and ideologies; though he admired her zeal, he disagreed with her perspective. Freda never envisioned dating a conservative, but has grown to appreciate his differing views on certain things. Al has a 6-year-old daughter, whom he gets to keep every other weekend, and he has a great relationship with his ex-wife and accepts equal blame in the failure of the marriage. The fact that he and Freda both are garage-sale junkies makes for very long and fun weekends, driving around the city looking for bargains. They enjoy each other's social circles, too; which, in turn, has helped to grow their own friendship. Al is a successful attorney with a busy schedule, but finds quality time to spend with Freda. Both being Catholic makes it easy to worship together, but where they go for breakfast after church is always a heated discussion.

They both like art and are frustrated painters. He paints landscapes and she paints portraits. Freda knows she has become a better person while dating Al, and believes they have built a strong foundation to establish a healthy relationship.

By looking at what has transpired with Freda and Al, you can see many positive characteristics of what healthy dating looks like. Here are some examples:

- He respects Freda's feelings and views, even when they are different.

- He is interested in getting to know her and wanted to hear what she had to say.

- He is nonjudgmental and appreciates the diversity they both represent.

- He is willing to explore their differences of opinion.

- He is responsible for a child from a failed marriage.

- He is financially responsible and can take care of himself.

- He accepts his role in the demise of his previous marriage.

- He likes her friends.

- He speaks about others in a supportive and kind way.

- He shares her interests, pastimes, and hobbies.

- He has similar religious beliefs.

- He has a good work life balance.

Al and Freda both possess many positive traits that you look for in someone you are dating. Here is a list of traits you want and traits you don't want in someone you are dating:

Traits You Want	Traits You Don't Want
attractive	emotionally unstable
open	insecure
responsible	drama king/queen
sensitive	obsessive
caring	manipulative
successful	whiney
not afraid of intimacy	helpless
emotionally open	lazy
can talk about feelings	immature
sense of humor	complainer

makes you feel appreciated	unreliable
healthy & fit	self-absorbed
faithful	deceptive
honest	negative
ready for commitment	selfish
empathetic	close-minded

MEASURE WHAT YOU TREASURE

In business, they say things that get measured get done; it's very difficult to manage something you can't measure. In business, a metric is any type of measurement used to gauge some quantifiable component of a company's performance, such as Return on Investment, (ROI). Measurements help businesses make better business decisions. The ROI in relationship economics is, benefits received for the time, energy, and effort invested in dating.

There could be many benefits received from dating, such as friendship, companionship, relationship, or marriage. One of the measurements of a healthy business is cash flow; in romance, cash flow equals quality dating partners.

In romance, dating is King, and in order to have positive cash flow, you have to date more quality partners than losers; and in order to have a profit, you must have a healthy relationship; and in order for you to have a high return on investment, you have to receive a benefit (marriage) that reflects the amount of time and energy you invested in the relationship (cost).

The metric you will use to determine if your dating partner has what it takes to potentially be worthy to be in a relationship with you is the N.I.C.E. Model. After a series of dates (5-10), you need to measure him on these four characteristics:

Nice = Kind + Cooperative + Warm-hearted
Intelligent = Bright + Creative + Knowledgeable
Compatible = Fun + Good Communication + Shared Values
Emotionally Stable = Relaxed + Patient + Optimistic

You can develop your own model to measure your partner, but this model is built upon the principle that you should only date someone NICE.

If you experience chronic confusion with the dating process or with the person you are dating, and you feel you are getting "mixed signals," you are most likely not in a healthy dating situation with long-term potential. You may want to have a crucial conversation with your partner, to determine if there is a possibility of developing a relationship.

FROM DATING TO A RELATIONSHIP

How do you know when you're crossing the line from dating to a relationship? When is it time to take dating to the next level? When do you know it's time to move in together? Why should you get married? These are very simple, but complex questions; one of the reasons they are complex is because women don't always know where they stand with their partner; are you just friends, are you dating, are you in a relationship?

Instead of asking a partner where they are in the relationship and where it is going, some women just hope things will work out for the best. Hope is not a strategy; it's a wish in your heart for something good to occur. Casinos and lotteries are built on hope.

If you truly are looking for a life partner and want a loving, lasting, healthy relationship, then you have to understand when you are actually in a relationship. A romantic relationship represents much more than an occasional good time or an evening of sexual bliss.

When you feel that the man you are dating, seeing, hanging out with is the only person you want to see, then you need to have a crucial conversation to find out if he is feeling the same way. A relationship is a mutual agreement between two people who have decided that they are going to be **exclusive**, **monogamous**, and **committed**. Now it is very important that you and your partner agree on what each of these words mean. Men have a tendency to have different meanings for these words. So understand that just because a man says he understands, it doesn't always mean what you think it means. To help in the discussion with your partner, here are definitions for these words:

Exclusive – You are not seeing anyone else romantically or looking for anyone else romantically, you will not date other people. **Monogamous** – You have only one sexual partner, you are faithful sexually to your partner, you do **not** engage in any form of sexual expression with anyone but your partner. **Committed** – You are willing to work on making and keeping the relationship healthy, you are making your partner a priority and not looking for other options.

TAKE A STAND OR YOU WILL TAKE A FALL

Ladies, if you don't take a firm stand on what your definition is of a committed relationship, you will fall for anything your partner wants it to mean. Romantic relationships can be difficult and complex because each one is different. In romance, feelings are strong and personal. Regardless of how together you think you are, it is easy to feel hurt, rejected, and disappointed.

To be in a committed relationship, you and your partner have to have an understanding of the facts, which are 1) you have an exclusive sexual and emotional attachment, and 2) you have an attitude that is aligned with preserving the health of the relationship, by demonstrating care, respect, and trust.

The level of commitment gradually increases as the relationship grows and matures. Do not get into a relationship with a man who is not thoroughly immersed in the concept and the execution of exclusivity and monogamy. A man who is lukewarm in his enthusiasm of being with you, and you only, is the wrong partner; you need to pass on him and don't give him any more romantic time.

MEN CAN BE STUPID

There are two concepts that men have embraced and demonstrated that have made it difficult for women to be in healthy relationships. Not every man you encounter is a proponent of these concepts. Therefore, I don't want to paint a picture and use such a broad brush that I indict every warm-blooded male; but since I am writing this book for women, I am compelled to share this with you.

Concept 1 is when a man wants the best of both worlds. It's called, **"He wants to have his Kate and Edith, too."** He wants to have Kate, his loving partner, with whom he shares his social life. She takes care of most of his emotional needs and puts up with his shortcomings and idiosyncrasies; in other words; his crap. But she stays by his side and is always there to figuratively pick up the pieces and literally pick up his dirty laundry.

Then there is Edith, the hot office romance, chick-on-the-side, late-night booty call, or whatever you want to call her, who brings out his beast. She makes him feel young, full of life, and allows him to walk on the wild side. She may not be good enough to be his "woman," but she is bad enough to be the "other woman." When a man is given a choice between two mutually exclusive desirable things, he can't have them both; and if he tries to have them both; eventually he will lose one and end up despising the other. You have to make sure that your partner is ready for a serious relationship and is not trying to have his Kate and Edith, too.

Concept 2 is called **"Married Single."** This is when a man who is married or in a "committed" relationship wants to act like he is single. This is the man who when asked if he is married, responds, "No, I'm not, but my wife is." He said I do, but he meant I won't. He won't stop living the single life, he won't stop dating other women, and he won't honor his marriage vows. He carries his wedding ring in his pocket when he goes out; often forgetting to put it back on when he comes home to the wife. She notices it and asks, "Where is your ring? And he states, "Oh, I was washing my hands and put it in my pocket." This kind of man will bring you dark days and take the shine out of your light. Make sure when you pick that permanent partner, he does not want to be "married single."

A romantic relationship is fundamentally a reciprocal emotional connection between you and your partner; and you have to make sure you both are emotionally prepared to be exclusive, monogamous, and committed to each other and the relationship.

HOW TO KNOW IF YOU ARE READY FOR A ROMANTIC RELATIONSHIP

To go from dating to a committed relationship is not always an easy decision to make. It isn't fair to you or your partner to begin a relationship and not be sure if you are ready or able. Here are seven ways to check and see if you are ready for a relationship:

1. You are happy with who you are and comfortable in your own skin. If you are not happy with yourself, how can you expect anyone else to be?

2. You are happy being single, you recognize it's not a curse but a choice, and a person or a relationship does not define who you are or determine your state of mind.

3. You have put closure to past relationships and past partners. You are over your ex and look forward to starting a new relationship. You cannot move forward if you live in the past. Unresolved feelings can put a strain on a new relationship.

4. You acknowledge that a life with Mr.Good4U is a life worth living and enjoying.

5. You are honest enough with yourself to know if you are ready to do and to be all the things necessary to be part of a healthy and happy relationship.

6. You no longer want to date other people. You want to focus your efforts and romantic energies on one person.
7. You will commit the time it takes to maintain and grow a healthy relationship. Not being available physically can lead to being unavailable emotionally.

FROM DATING TO COHABITATING

A story: Odessa and Larry started dating 10 months ago. Odessa is a CPA at a large accounting firm. Larry is an ex-professional football player, who is disabled due to a chronic neck and back injury sustained from his six years on the gridiron. The injury has made it difficult for Larry to find sustainable employment. They both are 53, and each has a failed marriage. Odessa is the primary wage earner and pays the majority of the household expenses. Three months ago, Larry moved in with Odessa. It was his idea; and after two months of trying to convince her it would be a good move, she agreed; Odessa was hesitant at first, because she was hoping they would get married. Larry has mentioned to her that this arrangement is temporary, and they will get married when he is more financially stable. During dates, Odessa noticed that Larry took a variety of prescription pain medicine, which altered his mood; his erratic behavior sometimes frightens her. Odessa's adult sons don't like Larry. They rarely come to the house and this saddens her. Odessa's friends have been telling her that Larry is using her for her finances and never intends to marry her. Two weeks ago, she brought the marriage subject up and Larry got angry. He grabbed her arm in anger, admonishing her to get off his back. Odessa is torn between her love for Larry and her concern for her own safety and emotional well-being.

A story: Erica and Dante are both 26-year old attorneys, fresh out of law school. Recently, Erica passed her bar exam and is currently working for a law firm. Dante is clerking at a law office and is studying to take the bar exam next month. After two years of being in a committed relationship, Dante suggested that they get a loft together. Erica was thrilled, but knew it would not go over well with her parents. One Sunday dinner at Erica's parents' home, Dante told them that Erica and he were moving in together, but he shared with them that his intention was to marry their daughter. While neither parent stood up and applauded, they appreciated the candor and transparency. If all goes according to plan, he will propose to her within the next six months and be married nine months later.

What these examples show are the two sides of shacking up, living in sin, or cohabiting; no matter what it's called, it's on the rise in this country. Census Bureau figures show that 4 million couples are living together outside of marriage, eight times as many as in 1970.

Odessa/Larry and Erica/Dante represent the two types of cohabitation arrangements: those in which the partners intend to marry, and those in which they do not.

Larry probably never had any intentions of marrying Odessa, but cohabiting presented an opportunity to live rent-free and enjoy other amenities. Erica and Dante moved in with the sole purpose of being married in the near future.

Some couples prefer cohabitation, because it does not legally commit them to an extended period, and because it is easier to establish and dissolve without the legal costs often associated with a divorce. Partners who cohabit with the intention of marrying share many of the characteristics of married people.

Those who cohabit without the intention of marrying often have short relationships with few benefits.

Larry tells Odessa he will marry her when he is ready. Only 30 percent of couples who live together actually get married. Erica and Dante think that living together will give them a better chance of staying married; when in actuality the dissolution rate for couples who lived together before marriage is 80 percent higher than it is for couples who didn't.

Odessa expressed concerns for her safety living with Larry; and she should. Out of 100 couples living together. 35 experienced a physical assault in a 12-month period; that's more than double the rate of violence among married couples, which is 15 out of 100. Odessa should also be concerned, because men who live with their girlfriends before marrying them are more likely to be underemployed than men who have not cohabited.

I am not sure why so many people, young and old, are choosing to cohabit. All the facts and statistics show that cohabitation is linked to poorer marital communication, lower marital satisfaction, higher levels of domestic violence, and a greater chance of divorce.

People who cohabit often contend that marriage is just about a piece of paper. Studies reveal, however, that there is quite a bit of difference between being married and living together. It's possible that if you feel the need to "test" the relationship, you may already know in your heart of hearts that it's not meant to be. What happens if you fail the test? You pack up your bags and go home...Oops that was your home.

If you graduate from dating to cohabiting, here are some things to think about:

- Do you really know each other well enough?

- Is the relationship foundation strong enough to withstand 24/7 together?

- Have you had disagreements/conflict and worked it out agreeably?

- Have you taken vacations together and enjoyed it?

- Have you discussed how finances will be handled?

- Are you prepared to give up your personal space?

I BEG OF YOU

My successful, sassy, single women, if you don't get anything else out of this chapter or this book, please, I beg you, remember this and never forget it. Your failure to follow this has put you on your knees in tears and in prayer wondering what, why, and how is this happening to me? Departing from this sage advice has caused those terrible twins (trauma and drama) to enter into your home and life.

Ladies, after you read this repeat it three times in the mirror. Promise me you will. Go to the nearest mirror right now and say. **"I will only date men who are <u>worthy</u> of being in a relationship with me."**

You have spent too many hours, days, weeks, months and yes, even years, dating men who didn't have the potential for a meaningful relationship. I am not saying you should only date to find a marriage partner, but I am saying you will never soar like an eagle by wasting your time with turkeys.

If you view dating as a discovery phase, to identify who is worthy to be in a relationship with you, and you understand the importance of your time and the value of your gift, and you treat it as the treasure it is, you are paving a smooth road on the journey to finding your life partner.

Yesterday is history,
Tomorrow is a mystery,
Today is a gift, that's why we call it the Present.
Answer the following dating questions:

1. Describe what you consider a successful first date?

_____

_____

2. What do you look for on a first date?

_____

_____

3. What do you hope to discover about your date?

_____

_____

4. Do you think you are an interesting person to date? Why or why not?

_____

_____

5. How long would it take you to decide you want a second date?

_____

_____

6. If the date is going poorly, what would you do?

_____

_____

Fill in the percent you think each quality represents what dating is about (it should add up to 100%)

say it's about love _____
marriage _____
sex _____
romance _____
friendship _____
partnership _____
sharing _____
company _____
social life_____
conversation _____

7. How many dates do you need before you decide you want to be in a relationship?

_____

_____

8. When it comes to dating are you old school or new school? Explain why.

_____

_____

9. Do you flirt on the first date? If so explain how.

_____

_____

10. What are you dating boundaries?

_____

_____

Your next date may be your permanent mate. Take dating seriously, and date men who are already happy, well-adjusted, kind, considerate, love their mother and are NICE.

CHAPTER SEVEN
YOU ARE THE PRODUCT

FEATURES AND BENEFITS

In a company, the strength of the product forms the foundation for the entire business; product is key. To be successful in business, you must have a strong product. Products are created to sell to other businesses (business-to-business, B2B) or to consumers (business-to-consumer, B2C).

What does it mean to have a strong product? It means people want what you have Nike, Apple, Microsoft, McDonalds, and Starbucks. All have strong products, because people feel they must have them. Strong products should be a solution to some problem.

Customers expect products to perform in a way that satisfies their needs. Expectations are driven by past experiences and whatever the customer believes is success.

Products consist of features, benefits, functions, and uses; they can be tangible or intangible.

A feature tells what the product has; a benefit tells what the product does, specifically, for the customer. I have never heard of anyone wanting to buy acetaminophen (the main ingredient in Tylenol), which is the <u>feature;</u> but people will buy it for relief of aches and pain, which is the <u>benefit</u>. People do not buy products; they buy the benefits the product offers.

Having been in sales the majority of my adult life, I have firsthand knowledge of the importance of product knowledge. Here are some reasons for the importance of product knowledge:

- Able to present the product and answer any questions related to it with confidence and enthusiasm, you are better at persuading customers to buy your product. It develops confidence in selling.

- Customers see your confidence and product knowledge; they will also appreciate the effort made in telling them about the important features and benefits of the product. It builds customer relationship and trust.

- Able to recommend a suitable product to your customer; reduces the chances of customer being unhappy. You match the right product with customer's needs.

- Able to explain better, demonstrate all the features of the product, and highlight its benefits to customers. Allows you to make a better sales presentation

It is understood that if you **do not** know your product, you cannot sell it.

When it comes to romantic relationships, you are the product. Features describe you; benefits describe the results your partner will receive being in a relationship with you.

How well do you really know your product? What is the reality of who you are? Are you a mother, daughter, niece, sister, aunt, ex-wife, and girlfriend? Who are you really? When you go beyond these labels, what are you left with?

If we strip away your professional position, your Nordstrom's charge card, your good looks, your pretty smile, your hair (store-bought counts, too), would you recognize yourself in the mirror? You should always feel comfortable and proud with the image that you see staring back at you in the mirror because of what you are made of.

Have you ever spent time by yourself, examining your internal makeup, your moral compass, and your values, and then ask if the real you is showing up when you meet a partner?

Is the real you still there inside, but scared to come out?

Being authentic means to be true to your own personality and spirit, despite the pressures from external forces and influences, like men, family, and friends.

In this chapter, you will go through an intense, in-depth introspection, to find out who you really are, what you stand for, why you are the way you are. After finishing this chapter, you will be able to label your product package **"new and improved."**

In writing this book, I like to think of myself as a truth speaker; saying things with the express purpose of making a difference in the lives of successful, sassy, single women who want to find the right man. In order to be true to this statement, I have to share an observation about some of you.

There are a number of you reading this book who are looking for a mate, and you are confused as to why you have **not** been able to find the right one; there are reasons, and here are a few of them:

- You are too angry.
- You don't take good care of yourself physically.
- You are boring.
- You drink too much hater-aide (jealous juice).
- You want to tear a man down, not build him up.
- You major on minors.
- You come off as cold and uncaring.
- You complain and whine too much.
- You have a lot of stinking thinking.
- You need to relax and take it down a notch.

Now that you recognized some of your girlfriends in the list, and agree that they need to stop some of that behavior, we can talk about you and what it takes to prepare you—the product.

Preparation entails making sure that you are mentally, spiritually, and emotionally prepared to start dating and to be in a committed healthy relationship. In order for you to be right for someone else, you first have to be right for you.

What are you doing to be at your maximum level of effectiveness in all areas of your professional and personal life? In order to attract a partner who is emotionally whole and authentic, you must come to the relationship whole, well, functioning, and emotionally balanced.

In a healthy relationship, your partner is not there to take care of you or fix you, just like it is not your job to fix him. He can support you emotionally and when needed, be the strength you need to lean on; but it's not his job to fill in what you are lacking and make you happy. In what areas might you be lacking right now? In addition, what can you do to improve those areas? Is it lose a few extra pounds and get fit, strengthen your self-confidence, start your own business, learn a foreign language, drop that loser of a partner you have now. Whatever the case, there is no time like the present to work on loving you some you. Learn to love and take care of yourself before entering into a relationship.

When you feel good about yourself, it shows and others see and feel it, too.

TO KNOW YOU IS TO LOVE YOU

The playwright Oscar Wilde said, "To love oneself is the beginning of a lifelong romance. In order for you to be the best product (person) you can be, and maximize your human potential, you have to have self-love and self-knowledge.

Self-love is that inner peace that reflects an awareness of who you are, what you have to offer, and your value as a wonderful child of the King. No one can give to someone else what they do not possess. If you don't love yourself, then it is difficult to love someone else.

Self-knowledge is knowing yourself intimately. It involves knowing your thoughts and feelings, how they came about, and how they influence your behavior; it is about understanding your needs, desires, motivations, beliefs, views, and values.

Self-knowledge is important, because it helps you to understand yourself better. Through self-understanding, you are in more control of your own life and better positioned to be an asset in your partner's life. You then have more influence in making life happen **for** you rather than have life happen **to** you.

Through self-love and self-knowledge, you create self-awareness, which is a way to explore your personal beliefs, baggage, and behaviors.

Self-awareness is important. When you have a better understanding of who and what you are, you are empowered to challenge yourself to grow and improve, reinforce strengths, eliminate weaknesses, and learn how your actions affect others.

When it comes to romantic relationships, self-knowledge is being aware of your thoughts, ideas, and feelings about love, romance, intimacy, men, and relationships, as well as how you developed those thoughts and how they influence your behavior.

Develop a relationship with yourself before getting deeply involved with anyone else.

Answer the following questions:

1. What are your likes and dislikes?

_____

_____

_____

2. What makes you feel guilty, and why?

_____

_____

_____

3. Do you feel angry and bitter at yourself and others? Why or why not?

_____

_____

_____

4. Do you play the blame game? Why?

_____

_____

_____

5. Who really irritates you? Why?

_____

_____

_____

6. What gives you simple pleasure?

_____

_____

_____

7. What are your unique talents and gifts?

_____

_____

_____

8. What gives you passion? Why?

_____

_____

_____

9. Do you feel stuck? Why or why not?

_____

_____

_____

10. Do you feel comfortable and safe when you are alone?

_____

_____

_____

11. Do you feel successful, and what do you define as success?

_____

_____

_____

12. Do you like working alone or as a team player, and why?

_____

_____

_____

13. Are you codependent in relationships?

_____

_____

_____

14. Do you love yourself unconditionally? Explain.

_____

_____

_____

15. What are your desires and ambitions?

_____

_____

_____

16. Do you feel special? Why or why not?

_____

_____

_____

17. Do you feel you need a man in your life? Why or why not?

_____

_____

_____

18. Do you rely on others for guidance, if so, whom?

_____

_____

_____

19. What do you admire most about men?

_____

_____

_____

20. What is your contribution to make this a better world?

_____

_____

_____

BELIEFS, BAGGAGE, AND BEHAVIORS

A story: Nicole is a 37-year-old flight attendant, who recently ended a three-year relationship with Manuel. The breakup was unexpected and caused Nicole to be both angry and bitter. She thought Manuel was the one; and he turned out to be just another one, who has disappointed her and altered her dreams. During their time together, he always commented when he saw an attractive woman, and verbally complimented the body part he felt was exceptional. Though curvy, Nicole wasn't endowed with large breasts, something Manuel seemed to be enamored with on other women. This, along with what she calls a boring sex life, has left Nicole feeling unattractive and somewhat scarred by the memories of Manuel mentally comparing her to other women. With her self-esteem at an all-time low, Nicole is in no hurry to start dating again and leery of getting back into a relationship.

Nicole is currently having negative thoughts and feelings about herself and her romantic future. These thoughts could cause her to behave in certain ways, which might not help her in her next relationship.

Nicole is now in a group, which some men call the "walking wounded." These are women who've been hurt by men in the past and carry emotional pain and unresolved anger into new relationships.

No matter what or who caused the wound, the romantic lives of the walking wounded are steered by their damaged psyches and bruised egos. Women like Nicole need time to heal and regain their emotional equilibrium and self-confidence.

Without acknowledging the psychological effects the relationship with Manuel has caused her, Nicole could spiral into destructive patterns of self-deceit and self-sabotage. She could become blind to her negative behavior and its consequences in her life.

WHAT ARE YOUR BELIEFS

Answer the following questions by finishing the sentence:

1. I think relationships are

   _____

2. My partner must

   _____

3. Men in general are

   _____

4. Relationships fail, due to

   _____

5. When it comes to men, I

   _____

Positive or negative expectations are formed by your beliefs; expectations can also be formed by conditioning. For example: If you have not had success dating tall men, in addition to forming negative beliefs about tall men, you also can get conditioned to expect to not do well dating tall men, in the future. If you magnetize your mind with limiting or negative beliefs, it becomes a magnet. The magnet not only pulls you to partners who reinforce those negative beliefs, but also it pushes those partners to you.

Here are some examples of limiting beliefs:

- If you believe that you aren't good enough to be in a healthy, loving relationship, you will be attracted to men who are incapable of loving you. These types of men will also be attracted to you. When you get into a relationship with this man and he doesn't love you, then you have reinforced that negative belief that you aren't good enough to be in a loving relationship.

- If you believe men are dogs, how will that influence your choices in selecting a partner? You probably will be attracted to a man for a particular reason and wait for a behavior that would allow you to declare him a bow-wow. Maybe because you believe he is a certain way, you act a certain way, which brings out the quality you expected.

- If you believe you are not attractive enough to connect with the kind of man you desire, you will act in ways that may not be attractive to that man. If you start acting like a beautiful woman, then you are a beautiful woman; and if that man doesn't recognize you, it's his loss.

Here are some limiting belief statements:

- "If I get in a relationship, I know I will get hurt again."

- "I will never find love; it's too late for me."

- "I'm too busy to find a partner."

- "All the good men are taken."

- "Men can't help themselves from cheating."

- "I would get into shape, but for what, no man wants me."

- "My partner should know what I want, I shouldn't have to ask."

- "The reason I am angry is because men made me this way."

- "All relationships are doomed to fail."

UNPACK YOUR SUITCASE

Your body carries your life experiences and your emotional turmoil. It's called baggage. While we all carry some emotional baggage, it turns out that some of us carry quite a few more bags than others.

Past relationship baggage can adversely affect present and future relationships, unless you learn how to successfully unpack the baggage and leave it in the past where it belongs.

I know that as a successful, sassy, single, high-powered sex machine, you would not want to classify yourself as a soldier in the walking wounded brigade; but just to double-check; here are ways to know for sure if you might have enlisted and didn't realize it:

You have not been able to overcome the memories and thoughts of your old boyfriend. You still have hopes that you will get back with him. You compare all other partners to him; and very few, if any, have been able to live up to the lofty standard he has set. It's amazing that, after the breakup, you only remember the good things about your ex and forget some of his flaws. There is a reason he is an ex.

You are paranoid that the new relationship will turn out badly, and you take out of context any and every little situation. You create mountains out of molehills, and major on the minors. A woman who assumes she will be hurt cannot trust anyone, and trust is the core of any relationship. Most men will not stick around when a woman acts like Chicken Little and everyday believes the sky is falling.

You think, act, feel, and speak like a victim. There are no guarantees in a relationship. You entered under your own free will; therefore, you have to accept the results. If a relationship fails, there is usually enough blame to go around. Most men aren't attracted to a woman who always sings that somebody done me wrong song. Quality men don't like a Lady who sings the Blues.

You are angry and bitter and take it out on all men, even your man. People deal with pain in different ways, oftentimes people who are hurting hurt others, even the ones they love. Don't make a man guilty of a crime that he didn't commit.

A quality man is willing to help his partner with her emotional baggage; but if the baggage resembles the whole Samsonite Company, then it would probably not be to his emotional best interest to stay in the relationship.

Everyone comes to a relationship with an emotional suitcase or garment bag; but they need to lose that baggage, or at least manage it, in order to have a healthy relationship. You can't move your life forward and engage in future successful relationships, until you can put down that emotional baggage that you are dragging around.

PATTERNS OF BEHAVIOR

A story: Essie is a 41-year-old financial planner, divorced twice, and currently in a toxic relationship with John, a 46-year-old civil servant. Like her two husbands, John is abusive and very controlling. Essie's friends don't understand how such a smart woman ends up with such bad partners. When dating, Essie always sees the good in a person and rationalizes away their faults. Essie believes she has many frailties and flaws of her own, so who is she to judge them. Even when it has become obvious to her that a potential suitor is unsuitable, she has not walked away from the relationship. Having been raised in a home where her father was verbally abusive, Essie has accepted the same kind of man as her father. Thinking she will change these men, she has put herself through painful and humiliating situations. Realizing John is not adding to her quality of life, she is contemplating breaking it off with him; but after two years invested in the relationship, she is questioning if that would be the right move.

We hear stories like Essie's and wonder how she, as well as others, keeps ending up with the same type of man. The truth is, changing habits or patterns of behavior are not easy; sometimes the chains of habit are too weak to be felt, until they are too strong to be broken.

When we look at Essie's pattern of behavior in accepting the wrong partner, we see a repetitive mode that may have been created by denied pain from her childhood. Though it may be obvious to others that she is picking the wrong type of man, this could be a blind spot that she can't see.

Patterns include both how you see the world and how you behave in it. One reason that Essie does not change is because she does not understand the foundation upon which the behavior patterns are built. Without this understanding, Essie's patterns of behavior become like a prison cell, locking her into poor choices and unwise decisions when it comes to picking a partner.

Essie has searched and not found the right partner. Even after two failed marriages, she still accepts men with the same characteristics. Essie, like other women with similar patterns, has to examine her personal shortcomings to see why she is accepting these types of men. The following are patterns that could be causing women to start and stay in relationships that are not good for them:

1. **Low Self-Esteem Patterns.** This is when you think you are no good and that no one would want you; therefore you have to put up with your partner's abusive behavior. Symptoms are:

   - Difficulty making decisions
   - Whatever you do, you think it isn't good enough
   - Embarrassed to receive praise and recognition
   - Don't let others know your needs aren't being met
   - Expect others to provide you with a sense of safety and security.

2. **Compliance Patterns.** This is when you compromise your own values and integrity to avoid a partner's rejection. Symptoms are:

- Extremely loyal, remain in harmful situations too long
- Value others' opinions and feelings more than your own
- Settle for sex when you really want love
- Make decisions without regard to the consequences
- Give up what you know to be true to gain approval from others.

3. **Avoidance Patterns.** This is when you act in ways that invite others to reject, shame, or express anger toward you. Symptoms are:

- Avoid emotional, physical, or sexual intimacy as a means of maintaining distance
- Use indirect and evasive communication to avoid conflict or confrontation
- Believe displays of emotion are signs of weakness
- Withhold expressions of appreciation
- Build a wall around your emotions, feelings, and heart

4. **Denial Patterns.** This is when you have difficulty identifying what you are feeling. Symptoms are:

- Minimize, alter, or deny how you truly feel about things
- Lack empathy for the feelings and needs of others
- Do not recognize the unavailability of men to whom you are attracted
- Are passive-aggressive
- Negatively label others

Each of these behavior patterns has emotions connected to it. If behavior patterns are going to change, the feelings that are associated or connected to them must be recognized, explored, and released. There are a variety of other behavior patterns that you may be displaying, which are preventing you from being in a healthy relationship. Without taking an introspective inventory of your personal strengths and weaknesses, you may repeat these unproductive behaviors.

Essie has to come to the realization that she needs to change some behavior patterns. This is not always easy; most change efforts **are not** pain-free. To help you in your quest to find the right man, answer the following questions:

1. List the behavior pattern(s) that you want to change

_____

_____

2. List your beliefs about that behavior(s)

_____

_____

3. List the feelings connected to the behavior(s)

_____

_____

4. List the benefits of giving up the old pattern and replacing it with a new one

_____

_____

HOW DID I GET THIS WAY?

A story: Kelly moved in with Ernie after only six months of dating. The whirlwind romance confused her, because she had just been in a tumultuous relationship that had to end before one or the other ended up in the grave or the penitentiary. It seemed like Ernie was her knight in shining armor, and she thought they loved each other. After the second date, Kelly who was physically attracted to Ernie became carnally connected.

Not being sure why she allowed it to happen so quickly, confused her. Being a bartender at a popular sports bar affords Kelly the opportunity to meet lots of people, and she developed a group of close friends. After meeting Ernie, she began spending less time with these friends. Agreeing to move in with Ernie seemed to be a good move at the time, due to their spending so much time together; but after two weeks, it all started to unravel. He began to turn into her ex-boyfriend, with the verbal abuse and the sarcastic comments.

He was controlling, manipulative, and had a total disregard for any of her emotional needs. What happened? How did she fall for this kind of man again? She became despondent and depressed in the relationship, and allowed Ernie to dictate and control her moods and feelings. Not having the emotional strength to fight any longer, Kelly wonders if she is cursed when it comes to men. Is it just bad luck, or is she just plumb dumb? She wants to know how and when she became this woman she is today.

Like Kelly, some of you will look at your relationship behavior patterns and wonder how and when you developed them. Kelly did what some of you have done and are still doing, confusing love for neediness, physical attraction, or the desire to be rescued.

Was Kelly terrified to be alone or desperate to be in a relationship? How did she get out of an unhealthy relationship only to find herself returning to the same kind of person? Like Kelly, sometimes you get sexually involved and emotionally connected too soon, before you really get time to know who the person truly is.

You are forceful, decisive, and show leadership skills at your workplace; but when it comes to relationships, you don't exemplify the same qualities, and it's confusing and frustrating. How can you manage a team of people at work, but not one man at home?

Why do you hold people accountable at work, but allow him to get away with anything he wants at home? Why do you feel invincible at work and vulnerable at home?

When did this behavior start? Why does it continue? Will you be able to stop it?

As you grew from childhood to womanhood, your behavior patterns developed from four influences:

1) One past influence was the **models you saw**. They may be your parents, family members, friends, teachers, or preachers. You watched how they acted, and you wanted to act like them, even when it was not good for you. Observing dysfunctional relationship patterns of behavior may be influencing your decisions on picking a partner.

2) A second influence is the **roles you held** in your family. You may have been the parent to your siblings or even to your parents. You were expected to be the caretaker for other family members, the straight "A" student, the prom queen. The roles you learned as a child influence your present behavior.

3) A third influence is your **beliefs,** which are attached to your behavior patterns. You may have learned that all men just want one thing. You may have learned that men exist to serve you. You may have learned that you are a kind, caring person. Your beliefs affect your behavior.

4) A fourth influence is the way you learned to **cope with your life experiences** during your childhood. Did you create imaginary friends?

Did you put your hands over your ears and hope it would go away? Did you pretend to be somebody else? Did you learn manipulation is the only way to get your needs met?

VALUES

A story: Amber is a 24-year-old NBA cheerleader. A college graduate with a finance degree, she was raised in a small town, by a single father, who was the pastor of a Baptist church. Amber has dated Jeff since freshman year in college, and loves him dearly. Since becoming a cheerleader, her relationship with Jeff has become strained, because her behavior has changed dramatically. Like others in her profession, Amber has become fascinated with NBA athletes, and she has "gone out" with more than a few. Reared in the church and believing in its Christian teachings, Amber feels these "hookups" go against her core values, but she so desperately wants to fit into her new glamorous, fast-paced world. Knowing she has lost her moral compass, she is confused on how to balance her dual existence, Amber is embarrassed to look Jeff in the eye, and has grown distant.

Their once loving and intimate relationship is strained, and Amber fears she will lose the man that truly loves her. Amber is confused. She knows that scripture states, "A double-minded person is unstable in all their ways"; the conflict raging inside her is tearing her apart.

Your personal values tell who you are and who you are not. They are your private meanings. You inherit some of your values. You learn some values from influential people in your life. Values arise from temperament and experience, and are

182

reflected in your individual goals, relationships, personal possessions, and preferences.

Choosing your personal values, unlike many other decisions, does not have a single answer. There are multiple values that help define the life and relationship you want to have. Well-defined personal values help to avoid making choices that are contrary to the person you want to be. Your values become a clear set of guidelines for your words and actions, consistently moving you in the direction aligned with your vision statement.

When you have a blueprint to guide you, life and relationships become your choice, rather than directed by the decisions of others. Your values have a twofold purpose: 1) they help build and maintain your identity as a unique individual; and 2) they are the guiding force for the kind of relationship you will have.

Women like Amber, who forget their values, tend to be wandering generalities, bouncing from one thing to another or from one man to another, trying to find who they are.

Knowing your values helps you do the following:

- Follow a clear set of rules and guidelines for your actions. You're less likely to take the easy way out or chase after fleeting pleasures or dead-end relationships at the expense of your long-term goals and healthy relationships.

- Make good life decisions as well as decisions about men; good choices help you become the person you want to be.

- Find compatible people, places, and things that support your way of living.

- Live with integrity. Integrity means wholeness or completeness— a whole person is true to themselves and others.

Amber is unhappy and frustrated because her personal values are conflicting with her lifestyle. This is apparent in both relationships and careers when women are dating or doing work that is in direct opposition to their personal values.

Many men, including myself, are attracted to a self-sufficient, secure, and confident woman, who knows who she is, what she is about, and won't compromise her values for a man or a job.

The woman who knows herself and understands her needs, wants, and desires is better able to articulate those things to her mate, and has a greater chance of finding the right man.

Your personal values are like having your own personal code. This code is unique to only you, and will map out how you live, how you act, what you say, and what you think.

Your values will dictate whether you live in the dark or in the light, whether it's fight or flight, or whether you stay down or get up.

VALUES LIST

Balance	Worthwhile Relationships	Nonjudgmental
Compassion	Self-fulfillment	Love
Respect	Understanding	Courage
Consideration	Innovation	Family
Excellence	Lead by example	Honesty
Confidence	Authenticity	Acceptance
Focus	Health/Fitness	Trust
Growth	Discipline	Sincerity
Productivity	Devotion	Creativity
Integrity	Acceptance	Truth
Drive	Competence	Purpose
Persistence	Fairness	Friendship
Strength	Optimism	Passion

List 10 values that are most important for what you are now achieving in your life. You don't have to think about this too much. It is usually fairly accurate to write down quickly the values that come into your mind, when you think about what you are aiming to achieve in life, as well as in relationships, and the values you are holding behind that. You can add your own values that are not included in the list.

List your personal values:

        _____

        _____

        _____

        _____

        _____

        _____

        _____

        _____

        _____

Now place those values in order of importance to you.

        _____

        _____

        _____

        _____

        _____

        _____

        _____

        _____

        _____

HOW DO YOU STAND OUT?

Your Unique Selling Advantage (USA) is that one distinct appealing idea that sets your business apart from your competitors. It distinguishes your particular business in a positive manner. The USA is your secret sauce; it is what makes you special.

Your USA is the focal point around which the success and profitability of your business is built, and so you must be able to state it and fulfill it honorably and effectively.

Advantages could include factors like a broad range of product selection, superior customer service, highest quality, best prices, and so on. It's always stated in terms of the benefit it delivers to your customers.

Your USA may be expressed as a summary of what you do and how you do it better or differently than others. Often, a USA can be summed up in just a few words, which become something of an advertising jingle or catchphrase. Here are a few well-known examples:

Burger King – Have it your way

They build on the premise that it's easy for a customer to request changes. Benefit to the customer: Satisfaction. No hassles (for trying to change the standard burger offerings) and a hamburger that's just the way you like it.

Enterprise – Pick Enterprise. We'll pick you up.

While Avis made a name for itself with its "We're number two, we try harder" slogan, which emphasized customer service, Enterprise focuses on one key selling point, customer pick up. Benefit to the customer: Convenience. You don't have to worry about taking a cab or bother with finding some other way to get your rental car. It comes to you.

Bounty – The Quicker Picker-Upper

Many products, such as paper towels or toilet tissue, have similar qualities. Bounty makes their mark by saying that their product absorbs spills faster.

If you started a business, your USA would list all of the various strengths that you or your product possesses. It would include items that reflect either the operation of your business or the quality of your business, such as location, surroundings, price, value, or product knowledge. To capture market share and be viable, sustainable, and profitable, you need to differentiate or distinguish your business and products from your competitors. In other words, you need to make your business special in the eyes of your customers.

When it comes to relationships, we have identified that you are the product. With this being the case, what is your Unique Selling Advantage? What's the one thing that makes you different from any other single woman? Why should a man want to be in a relationship with you? Do you promise him great value, benefits, or partnership?

Why go through the trouble of creating a Unique Selling Advantage? You're competing for single men's limited attention. It is important to know in your mind and heart why you would make a great life partner.

Answer the following questions:

1. What are three things that are unique about you?

_____

_____

_____

2. What are three benefits of dating you?

_____

_____

_____

3. What are three nice things past partners have said about you?

_____

_____

_____

4. What are three not so nice things past partners have said about you?

_____

_____

_____

5. What proof do you have that you are a good potential life partner?

_____

_____

_____

6. If you were a consumer product, what would you be and why?

_____

_____

_____

7. A feature is what the product has; name five things you have that make you a good partner.

_____

_____

_____

8. A benefit is what you get from the feature, name 3 benefits a partner would get from your features.

_____

_____

_____

9. What do you believe are your best qualities?

_____

_____

_____

10. Name three things that were good about your last
    relationship.

_____

_____

_____

UNIQUE IS WHAT YOU SEEK

Now that you have a better understanding of who you are as a product (person); take all of your features, benefits, qualities, strengths, values, nonnegotiable standards of performance, and condense them into one clear, concise statement of why you are an ideal life partner.

This statement is similar to an "elevator speech," which gets its name from the idea that if you were on an elevator and someone asks you what you do, you should be able to tell them concisely and clearly what it is before you get to your specified floor.

Close your eyes, and imagine you are in an elevator with the man of your dreams. He looks good, smells good, talks good, is very interested in you; and then he asks you this question, "Why would you make a good wife?" Your answer will be your Unique Selling Advantage.

_____

_____

_____

_____

_____

_____

GETTING READY TO GET READY

The more you know about starting a business, the more power you have to form an organization that develops into a lasting source of income and satisfaction.

The more you know about yourself, the more power you have to form a romantic relationship that develops into a lasting source of happiness and satisfaction.

Knowing yourself means knowing your life values, your beliefs about romance, men, intimacy, your priorities, your moods, your habits, your passions, your faults, your past relationship failures, your desires, your fears, your boundaries, your limits, your nonnegotiable standards, what you like, what you don't like, and what your purpose in life is.

Someone will always be prettier and thinner.
Someone will always be smarter and funnier.
Someone will always be younger and healthier.
But they will never be <u>You</u>.

TIME FOR A CHANGE.

CHAPTER EIGHT
STRUCTURING THE RELATIONSHIP

LEGAL EAGLE

Entrepreneurs, like single women, are looking for a joyful, rewarding, profitable business/**relationship**. Maybe you feel compelled to start your business because you are unemployed, underemployed, or seeking a second career. To start a business— or start a relationship—you don't need a degree, diploma, or a certificate, but it definitely helps if you have the knowledge to operate it. One of the most important choices an entrepreneur makes when she starts her business is deciding the type of legal organization she selects for her company.

Many factors must be evaluated when choosing a form of business organization; what you decide will be based on your goals and objectives. Six common issues distinguish the different business types. They are **1) taxation, 2) liability, 3) risk and control, 4) continuity of existence, 5) transferability,** and **6) expense and formality.**

Different business types may be under the jurisdiction of the city, state, or federal government, depending upon the type of business you choose. The most common forms of business structure are Sole Proprietorships, Partnerships, Limited Liability Corporations (LLC), and Corporations. One type is not necessarily better than any other; it's just a matter of which structure best suits your business needs.

Before reviewing the advantages and disadvantages of each of these legal structures, answer the following questions, to assess your needs and help you decide which type of business is best for you.

1. To what extent are you personally able, and your family willing, to be responsible for business debts and financial losses?
2. What impact would your death have on the continuity of your business?
3. How easy would it be to transfer your business, or your interest in the business, to your heirs if you die unexpectedly?
4. If your personal goals or economic conditions should change, how easy would it be to liquidate the business?
5. How much information about you and your business are you willing to make publicly available?

FOUR BUSINESS STRUCTURES

Sole Proprietorship. This is the simplest, oldest, and most common form of business organization. Here you are all by yourself; no other owners or partners are involved. You own all the assets and are responsible for all the debts. In legal terms, you and the business are identical. You also have unlimited personal liability. If the business incurs debts that it cannot pay, creditors can claim not only the business assets but your personal assets as well. The business income is treated as your personal income. If you have substantial personal wealth, you may want to consider another form of business.

The Advantages and Disadvantages of <u>Sole Proprietorship</u>

Advantages:
- Low organizational start-up costs
- Greatest freedom from government regulations
- Owner with direct control
- Personal tax advantages
- Make all business decisions

Disadvantages:
- Unlimited liability
- Lack of continuity if you die
- Difficult to raise capital

Partnership. This is an association of two or more persons, who serve as co-owners in a business for profit. This structure is relatively free from government regulations and easy to set up. The relationship is consensual, and it is usually bound by a legal contract that defines the partnership agreement. Each partner is personally liable for all business deals and debts; and all partners are liable for wrongful acts and breaches of trust by any partner. The income of the business is taxed as each partner's personal income.

The Advantages and Disadvantages of Partnerships

Advantages:
- Low start-up costs
- Additional sources of financing
- Broader management and expertise base
- Limited government regulations

Disadvantages:
- Unlimited liability of each partner
- Difficulty in finding suitable partners
- Unresolved conflict among partners
- Lack of trust among partners

Limited Liability Corporation (LLC). This is a distinct entity that is a hybrid of a partnership and a corporation. The LLC has the same limitations on liability as a corporation; the owners, like shareholders of a corporation, are not liable for the debts, torts, or other civil liabilities of the LLC. An LLC must be a domestic corporation, and all shareholders must hold USA residency. Only one class of common stock can be issued, the corporation is limited to 35 shareholders, and the IRS allows you to choose whether to be taxed as a corporation or as a partnership.

The Advantages and Disadvantages of Limited Liability Corporation (LLC)

Advantages:
- Limited liability of stockholders
- Can issue limited stock
- Easier to set up than a full corporation
- Single taxation

Disadvantages:
- Closely regulated by state governments
- Form not recognized in all states
- Extensive record keeping required
- More expensive to form than a partnership

Corporation. This is a legal entity, formed under state statutes, that has rights and liabilities separate from the people who created it. Shareholders elect a board of directors, which sets policy and appoints officers to manage the company on a daily basis. A corporation has a potentially unlimited life of its own; and it is not dissolved by the death of a shareholder, director, or officer. The primary benefit of forming a corporation is that the personal liability of the shareholders is limited to the amount of their investment in the company. Corporations can raise capital by issuing stock, which represents ownership in the business. Once the corporation has been formed, its officers or directors must adopt by-laws that govern the operation of the company. Shareholder meetings must be held and minutes recorded.

The Advantages and Disadvantages of <u>Corporations</u>

Advantages:
- Limited liability of stockholders
- Can issue stock
- Easier to raise money
- A legal entity in itself

Disadvantages:
- Closely regulated by state and federal governments
- Double taxation
- Extensive record keeping required
- More expensive to organize

RELATIONSHIP PROFILES

To help put structure into your romantic relationships, I am going to use the four traditional business forms, to identify what your relationship profile is. Many women get concerned and confused as to what the next level is for her and her partner. These categories will give you clarity, validation, understanding, and direction with your relationships. We will describe the relationship forms as the following:

- Sole Proprietor = **Dating**
- Partnership = **Relationship**
- Limited Liability Corporation (LLC) = **Living Together**
- Corporation = **Marriage.**

SOLE PROPRIETOR

A story: Dottie is a 38-year-old police officer and single mother of a teenage son. Her job has her constantly interacting with males. She has gone out with fellow officers, but has decided she won't do that anymore. Dottie is a serial dater, who enjoys the variety of dating different men. Not wanting to be responsible to another individual for where she goes or what she does, Dottie keeps her partners at an emotional arm's length, and has yet to introduce her son to any of her suitors. In the last four years, she hasn't gone out with the same man more than four times. Her friends joke that if a man gets to a fifth date, he will end up her husband. It is easy for Dottie to compartmentalize her feelings and not get emotionally involved with partners. When partners express their feelings, she gets uncomfortable and begins to disconnect. She feels she has never misled anyone into thinking that they are in a relationship with her; but she acknowledges that some men do assume a relationship exists.

Dottie tells her friends she is not promiscuous; but rather, she is hormonally selective and quite in touch with her BOB (battery-operated boyfriend). Recovering from an abusive marriage, Dottie believes this social lifestyle is best for her, as she continues to heal from her emotional scars. In her mind, she is young and single, looking to mingle, and is committed to her personal pleasure, happiness, and peace of mind.

Dottie is a sole proprietor, which is the simplest relationship form. The focus is on individual needs; and the freedom to date whomever you want, whenever you want. It is important to be able to self-identify as a sole proprietor, or recognize a person who is one, so you can manage expectations and avoid confusion and potential conflict.

Characteristics of a Sole Proprietor:

- This person dates a variety of different people, often at the same time.

- They do not want to be responsible for someone's emotional equilibrium, based on what they do or don't do.

- They may take a superficial interest in your life, but generally, they don't know what's going on in your world.

- Rarely will they go out of their way to accommodate your wish, want, or desire; and if they do, they remind you of the sacrifice they are making.

- You know very little about this person, and they give you the impression they prefer it that way.

- They are good at flirting, but get nervous if you get too close—emotionally, that is.

- They have mastered the art of being purposely vague.

- You never get a sense of how they feel about you, other than when they are annoyed with you, because they make that quite obvious.

- Your conversations are short, sweet, and devoid of any mention of their personal feelings and emotions.

- They can be charming and engaging, which sends mixed messages of interest and attraction.

- They will spend time with you, have fun with you, even sleep with you; but act confused as to why you thought what you had was a relationship.

- This is the person to whom you profess your love, and they respond by saying, "Thank you."

- This person would be quite comfortable dating you numerous times, with no intention of ever having anything more than what you have right now.

- If you were honest with yourself, you would have to admit that you don't know any more about this person on Day 30, 60, or 90 than you did on Day 1.

- They are fans of dating but allergic to relationships.

- The sole proprietor is an individual who wants to be free from any emotional heavy lifting.

- They are only looking to date.

If looking for a relationship partner were like buying a car, the sole proprietor would be the person who walks the lot looking at different models, checking under the hood, but is not interested in taking a test drive. The sole proprietor answers all the salesperson's questions, makes it appear he or she is highly interested and looking like a buyer would; but at the end of the day, there was a lot of activity and no accomplishment.

The sole proprietor looks like they want to be in a relationship and even may act like they want to be; but the truth is, they just want to kick the tires.

If you are a sole proprietor and not looking to change your relationship status, you may want to inform a partner after a period of time, to eliminate the possibility of misinterpretations and misunderstandings.

If you recognize a partner is a sole proprietor, and you are not, you must immediately have a crucial conversation, asking the following questions:

- Are we in a relationship? If so, how would you describe it?
- What are your intentions concerning me?
- How do you feel about me?
- Are you seeing other people?

Two sole proprietors can have a great time together, because neither person is trying to take whatever they have to the next level. The neutral gear that the relationship started in makes it virtually impossible for the relationship to go forward or in reverse. There can be lots of revving of the engine (fun, sex), but you don't go anywhere, like a treadmill; you can work up a sweat, but find yourself in the same old place.

WARNING: The Surgeon General of Relationships has declared Sole Proprietors as potentially dangerous and hazardous to your emotional health.

PARTNERSHIP

A story: Constance and Gerald have been dating for six months. What started as a rocky first few dates has turned into something special. They enjoy the same things, have similar temperaments and have become great friends. Never having been in a committed relationship, Gerald has been pleasantly surprised by how Constance makes him feel. She gives him enough attention, without smothering him, and doesn't try to change some of his annoying ways—like his constant fixation on ESPN, hollering and screaming at the TV when a game is on, and his refusal to try different types of food. Constance was dating a couple of guys when she met Gerald, but after a few dates with Gerald, she stopped seeing them. Their mutual respect is the glue that has held them together during the dating process. Constance likes to talk about feelings and her emotions, which make Gerald somewhat uncomfortable. Since they are both schoolteachers, they share much in common and support one another. While she is 28, and he is 30, they have discussed the future and realized that either they are going to grow as a couple or slow down the pace. Gerald knows something is happening inside of him, emotionally, concerning Constance; the thought of her with another man makes him almost physically ill. He is realizing that it might be time to turn in his player card and settle down.

A primary difference between sole proprietor and partnership is that sole proprietors are not necessarily monogamous. With sole proprietors, a commitment is not required, and they are free to see other people at the same time that they are seeing you.

People involved in partnerships are monogamous; and therefore, each partner commits to only being involved with the other person. Constance and Gerald are ready to go from casually dating to being in a relationship. Remember, dating is not a relationship; it is a discovery phase, to try and find someone with whom to share a relationship.

Characteristics of a Partnership:

- After dating for a period of time, you realize there is something special.

- You want to take it beyond just casual dating.

- You are willing to make some sacrifices, in order to take it to the next level.

- You believe you have earned the right to ask the who, what, and where questions. Who were you with? What did you do? Where did you go?

- They have established a degree of trust with you, but it is conditional.

- You are comfortable in their presence and feel you can be 100 percent yourself.

- You like so many things about this person, the chemistry is definitely there, and the compatibility factor is growing.

- You feel like now is the time to introduce them to your family, but you will limit their exposure and access.

- You want to spend holidays with them.

- Their behavior is predictable and you enjoy that; you don't do well with someone who has a rollercoaster type of disposition.

- You enjoy the bonding process with them, and you can see the emotional fruits from the time you spend together.

- They make you realize how dysfunctional your last relationship was, because of the ease in which you two make conversation, decide on things, and agree to disagree, agreeably.

- You appreciate the manner in which they respect you and never put you in a position to feel unsafe.

- You have seen some flaws, but those are rough edges that you know you can smooth out.

- You are convinced that they could be a keeper, but you aren't sure you want to keep them forever. For right now, they are all of that and your personal bag of chips.

- You want to be 100 percent transparent, but something inside says withhold certain things.

- You want to make a commitment to this person.

If looking for a partnership was like buying a car, the partnership partner would be the person who walks the lot looking at different models, decides on the car they like, and takes it for a test drive. The test drive is designed to get a feel for the vehicle, how it performs and operates, and if the vehicle meets your expectations enough to purchase it.

Once you take your relationship form to partnership status, focus will be needed to assure both partners' needs are being met. Relationships require time, attention, and patience in order to grow and develop.

LIMITED LIABILITY CORPORATION

A story: Kiki recently opened up a deli with her best friend Tina. The store has opened to rave reviews and is packed at lunchtime most days. The success of the store has brought Kiki closer to Tariq, her boyfriend of three years, mainly because of the time they spend at the deli, where he is the kitchen manager. The relationship has been up and down, especially last year after Kiki admitted to having an affair. They worked hard on staying together. With the help of counseling, they have been able to survive the breach of trust and move forward. Spending so much time together at work, and such little time together outside of work, Kiki has been thinking about suggesting to Tariq that he move in with her. This would be a major commitment by both partners, especially with Tariq having partial custody of his 11-year-old son. Kiki has never married or lived with someone, so sharing her space 24/7 is a major decision; but her love for Tariq is growing, and she wants to take what they have to another level. The respect she has for his work ethic and commitment to excellence makes her want him around her all the time. Kiki feels their relationship and commitment to one another is strong enough to withstand the pressures of living together. She does not want to live with Tariq for convenience or for financial reasons; she is doing this because she feels this is the man she wants to marry.

A limited liability corporation (LLC) is when a person feels like they are ready to cohabit, shack-up, or live together with their partner. An LLC is very similar to a marriage, but does not have its legal structure. Both partners in an LLC must be committed to each other and the relationship.

Characteristics of Limited Liability Corporation (LLC):

- You are emotionally invested in your partner.

- They are pretty much everything you want in a partner.

- You are looking for a more substantive commitment.

- They are a major part of your life.

- Your life plans are meshed.

- You want to see how compatible you two can be.

- Your family is comfortable with them.

- You are acknowledged by others to be a couple.

- You are faithful and loyal.

- You feel like this is the next step to marriage.

- You no longer are weighing your options, thinking you can find someone better.

- In your mind, they are your significant other.

- The next step is an engagement ring.

- You are in love or an extremely heavy dose of like.

- You look forward to waking up in the morning next to them.

- You genuinely like who they are as a person.

If looking for a relationship partner was like buying a car, the LLC would be the person who walks the lot looking at different models, decides on the car they like, takes it for a test drive, and decides they will lease the car rather than buy it.

A healthy LLC relationship is composed of two healthy individuals. Both of you have to be aware of the challenges that living together can cause, and you must be committed to making the relationship work.

CORPORATION

A story: Lynn and Calvin decided to try marriage, after living together for two years. Both 45 years old and divorced, they felt the timing was right, their relationship was healthy, and they were committed to each other. Calvin's friends have been skeptical of Lynn's motives, because he is financially stable and she was swimming in debt when they met. No doubt, being with Calvin has improved her overall financial well-being, but she feels she has given him a lot since they met. Lynn has a teenage daughter, who calls Calvin daddy, and Calvin has spoken with an attorney about legally adopting her. Lynn feels more secure now that she is legally protected and has recourse if something goes wrong in the marriage. Calvin was encouraged to have Lynn sign a prenuptial agreement outlining what she would be entitled to, in case of a divorce; but he refused, not wanting to put a damper on the love he has for her.

Being a corporation is being in a marriage where you have a more meaningful commitment and stronger sense of purpose. Lynn feels safe, because being in a corporation gives her something that an LLC does not give her, legal protection. Lynn and Calvin are both responsible for, and responsible to, each other—emotionally, spiritually, physically, and legally. A corporation, unlike an LLC, is a transformative act, changing the way a man and a woman view each other, as well as how they see their present and their future.

Characteristics of a Corporation:

- You love each other unequivocally.

- You are willing to share each other's credit history and debts.

- You want a permanent partner.

- You agree on key issues dealing with family, faith, and finances.

- You fight fair.

- You have done your due diligence and are satisfied with the results.

- Your family and friends are comfortable with your partner.

- You agree on how to raise and discipline children.

- You are faithful and loyal.

- Your communication is good.

- You are great friends with a great friendship.

- You believe your marriage will last forever.

- You can live with partner's flaws.

- You have vacationed together, and it went well.

- You admire and respect your partner.

- You want to grow old with them.

If looking for a relationship partner was like buying a car, the corporation would be the person who walks the lot looking at different models, decides on the car they like, takes it for a test drive, and decides they want to buy it.

Living as a partner in a corporation is what most successful and sassy women desire. The other choices are not as advantageous. The joys of being a sole proprietor are exciting but limiting. Being a partner in a partnership is the beginning of a journey that might lead to finding a life partner. A partner in an LCC has its benefits but also has many adverse consequences, if the relationship fails.

KNOW YOUR STATUS
A story: Candace and Terrance have been seeing each other for eight months. They met at a church function, and have enjoyed both the fellowship and the friendship. Candace, at 29,

is a young widow, having lost her husband in Iraq. Terrance is 34 and never married. Recently, they attended one of Terrance's company functions, and upon introducing Candace to a co-worker, he called her his girlfriend, which took Candace by surprise. On the way home, she mentioned that she felt awkward being introduced as his girlfriend. Terrance responded that he assumed she was his girlfriend. Candace let him know, in no uncertain terms, that they were just friends.

She still wanted to date other people and, though she enjoyed his company, she was not in a relationship with him. Hearing her say that they were not in a relationship made Terrance feel sad, discouraged, and disillusioned.

It is critically important that you self-identify what your relationship status is. Are you a sole proprietor, who is just looking to date? Are you in a partnership, which means you are in a relationship? Are you in an LLC and cohabiting? Are you in a corporation, which means marriage?

Each structure has its behaviors, expectations, motives, and meanings. If you find that you are a particular status and your partner is another, it creates interesting dialogue and potential dilemmas.

The case of Candace and Terrance is a classic example of a sole proprietor seeing someone who was in a partnership status. The lack of communication caused much of this confusion, and easily could have been avoided, by both parties engaging in crucial conversation.

Knowing what relationship structures both you and your partner are currently in, will help you manage expectations, identify patterns of behavior, and determine compatibility.

RELATIONSHIP STRUCTURE QUESTIONS

1. Answering the following questions yes or no:
   - Are you tired of dating ? _____
   - Do you enjoy first dates? _____
   - Are you a good partner ? _____
   - Are you a serial dater? _____
   - Do you want to be married? _____
   - Would you cohabit? _____
   - Do men understand you? _____

2. Which relationship structure do you believe you are currently in? Check one.

   Sole Proprietor _____ Partnership _____ LLC _____ Corporation _____

3. Why do you think you fall under the structure you chose?

   _____

   _____

   _____

4. How long do you think you will be in that structure and why?

   _____

   _____

   _____

CHAPTER NINE
FOUR FACES OF EVE

THE TALE OF THE TYPES

Nobody likes to be labeled, stereotyped, or put in a category. As a successful, sassy, single woman, you don't necessarily like the idea of being slotted into a role. The culture we live in today dictates that we embrace certain roles, like gender roles. Gender roles are the way people act, what they do and say to express being a woman or a man. These characteristics are shaped by society. Gender roles vary greatly from one culture to the next, from one ethnic group to the next, and from one social class to another. Women's representation in popular culture facilitates the stereotype of the naïve, emotional, and domesticated female. This is portrayed through various forms of media, including movies and television.

I don't want to appear to be stereotyping, but I have identified four types of women that have completely different approaches, attitudes, and actions, when it comes to partners and relationships. My intent in describing these four types is for you to see if you self-identify. If you see yourself in one of these types, what can you do to change, if needed, or continue on the same path, while trying to be even better and more effective.

LOIS LANE EFFECT

Lois Lane is the fictional character in the *Superman* comics. She was a strong, assertive woman, who was in love with Superman, and had an annoyed tolerance toward Clark Kent. She was unaware that they were, in reality, the same person. Lois was captivated by the qualities displayed by Superman; he was faster than a speeding bullet, stronger than a locomotive, could leap tall buildings in a single bound, and was a real live hero. Clark Kent was a nerdy, ordinary, regular guy, who had a warm heart and a kind spirit.

The Lois Lane effect is when a woman can look beyond the Clark Kent human frailties of her man and see his inner hero; in simple terms it's making your man feel super. One of the key indicators for a man, in terms of how he feels about a woman, is how that woman makes him feel about himself. When a woman makes her partner feel like Superman, she is paving a smooth road to relationship success. Men want and need to know their woman appreciates their masculinity, their manliness, and their muscle.

When a woman makes a man feel super, it makes him feel better about himself. Making a man have confidence and pride in himself is a talent. Women who develop this talent will find that they get the best and the most from their man.

When a man has the respect of his woman, it actually makes him want to become a better man. When it comes to relationships, feeling respected is a huge issue for most men. Giving your partner respect means valuing them and their thoughts, feelings, and dreams. It also includes acknowledging them, listening to them, being truthful with them, and accepting their individuality and peculiarities.

A woman's approval of her man is a great motivator for him to always give his best effort in trying to please her and meet her needs.

From time to time, it's a good idea for you to look closely at the way you have treated your partners, and make sure that your actions accurately conveyed your true feelings. Can you honestly say that you have tried to make your man feel super? Maybe you didn't because you didn't know how; a woman would do better if she knew better.

Let's look at seven ways that the Lois Lane effect can make your man feel Super:

- **Give him attention.** Attention is important to men. Show him that you are attracted to him; men have insecurities just like women, and they need to know you find them sexy and appealing. Let him know all the special little things you love about him, such as the way he smells, the sound of his voice, his strong arms, the way he makes you feel when he kisses you, or the sound of his laugh. A man likes to be reminded of why you think he is super.

- **Tell him you're proud of him.** Let him know when he does something well, and how you admire his competency and his character. Share with him the qualities he has that give you confidence in him and allow you to trust him. They say the only difference between a man and a boy is the price of his toys. Every man, no matter how successful he may be, still wants and seeks the approval of his mother, and you represent the need for that feminine approval.

- **Take interest in his interests.** The royal road to a man's heart is to find out the things he treasures and to show interest in them. Show enthusiasm over things that he's enthusiastic about. Men can be very passionate about their sports, hobbies, and recreational activities; knowing you support him in these endeavors, makes him see how special you are. Allow him to teach you things he likes, without your acting bored or indifferent. When a man knows you care about the things he cares about, it makes him care more about you

- **Help him achieve his goals.** No man wants to climb to the top of the professional mountain, look down and there is nobody to share in the triumph. When a woman is willing to roll up her sleeves, kick off her heels and risk breaking a nail to help her man achieve his dream that makes him feel super. If you help your partner get what he wants in life, it usually will help you get what you want.

- **Listen to him.** There is no more important thing that you can do to make a man feel valued or important than listening to him, his point of view, his outlook on life, or his life plans. You don't have to agree with everything, just listen and try to understand. Don't depreciate his ideas, intelligence or initiative. A man can tell when you listen with your ears; but he can feel when you listen with your heart. The heart hears both the content and the intent.

- **Ask for his advice.** Men like the idea of you wanting their help or advice. When you share your concerns and listen to his input and when possible act upon it; it makes your man feel empowered and valued. We all know what they say about opinions, but when your man gives you his opinion, let him know it is appreciated. Not that you have to be in any danger, but when a man feels like he is saving a damsel in distress, it makes him feel like Superman.

- **Focus on his strengths.** I teach a management style that includes walking around and catching people doing something right, identifying it, recognizing it, and verbally rewarding it; when this is done, I assure you that behavior will be repeated. Verbalize things to him, like "I wouldn't change a thing about you" or "Nobody can make me feel as good as you." Brag about him to other people, even when he's not there. Compliment him on his special gifts and abilities.

TIP: The Lois Lane effect is not about oiling a man's ego or manipulating his machismo meter, it's about making him feel needed, valued, important, and respected.

TRAP: Sometimes women forget that a man needs to know he is appreciated by his partner. When a man doesn't get certain feedback or verbal acknowledgements from the person he wants to hear it from; it sometimes makes him seek to hear it from someone else.

FLORENCE NIGHTINGALE SYNDROME

Florence Nightingale is best remembered for her work as a nurse during the Crimean War, and her contribution to the reform of the sanitary conditions in military field hospitals. Nightingale is responsible for the transformation of nursing, from its disreputable past into a responsible and respectable career for women. Thousands of soldiers were saved because of the work of Florence and her nurses.

The Florence Nightingale syndrome is when a woman feels it's her job to nurse emotionally wounded men to health, and fix those who, for whatever reason, are broken.

I am not sure why, but I have known, and known of, many successful, sassy, fabulous, phenomenal women, who pick men that are totally wrong for them. One of the main reasons I was compelled to write this book was that I couldn't understand or figure out why smart women get into dumb relationships. Why do professional women who make great decisions at work make such bad decisions at home? Have you ever seen an ugly person holding hands with a very attractive person, and you scratch your head and ask how did that happen? I scratch my head, wanting to know why a woman, who would be most men's Ms. Right, becomes obsessed with a man, who should be most women's Mr. Wrong. A man, who is emotionally wounded, is someone who is addicted to work, alcohol, gambling, pornography, sex etc.; and is not equipped, prepared, or able to love you back.

The term "broken," to describe a man, is open for interpretation, and some might consider it insensitive of me to use such a term. I don't use it to define a man, who is on tough economic times, and his finances are low; a quality man could find himself in a situation like that, due to conditions and circumstances. When I refer to a broken man, I mean someone who has sustained emotional, attitudinal, and mental harm throughout their entire life—harm that **may not** be repairable.

The Florence Nightingale syndrome makes a woman believe it is her role, duty, and obligation to heal the emotionally wounded and fix those that are broken.

Some women buy into the Tammy Wynette song, *Stand by Your Man*, which says you should attempt to overlook a man's shortcomings and faults. A modern version of this is the female rapper Eve's song, *Ride-or-Die Chick*. This is a woman who will do anything her man needs her to do, even if her death is the ultimate fate of their relationship. She is down for both the bad and the good. Ride-or-die chicks give their man their last dollar, let him run up her credit card, stop their life because he's in jail, and accept the fact that he sleeps with other women.

Every man respects a woman who is loyal; but no quality man will respect a woman who doesn't respect herself, accepts a man's foolish antics and disrespectful behavior, and disregards her morals and standards to satisfy someone else. When does helping your man cross over into hurting yourself? There have to be limits. Loving someone unconditionally doesn't include hurting yourself. Unconditional love is a term that means to love someone, regardless of their actions or beliefs. That should apply to your family, because no matter what your father or mother does, they will still be your father or mother; in these scenarios, you try to forgive and move on. But when a boyfriend does something to harm you or put you in harm's way, there is no legal or moral reason you have to stay.

Don't think that ride-or-die chicks are just those who live in a thug world. There are professional ride-or-die chicks, who accept mistresses and down-low arrangements to continue their status in the community or the country club.

Here are some different reasons why smart women do dumb things, like play nurse to a man broken into emotional and psychological pieces:

- Lonely and would rather have a broken man than no man at all

- Low self-esteem; feeling that she doesn't deserve a quality man, so she accepts the loser
- Profoundly spiritual, she believes this is her answered prayer and God has sent this man for her to fix
- Fearful of leaving him because of negative repercussions
- Belief that giving her all to one man will eventually make him her husband
- Naiveté, thinking he will change if she just loves him more, better, or harder.

Everyone, at sometimes in their life, needs a helping hand; but some people need more than a hand, they need professional help. The Florence Nightingale syndrome appears to be a noble and just affliction, but it often leads to supporting a man who chooses not to support you, assuming financial responsibilities for a man who is not responsible, and tolerating a grown man's childish antics and actions.

Frederick Douglas said, "It is easier to build strong children than to repair broken men."

> **TIP:** Many adults still have emotional scars and unhealed wounds inflicted early in their lives; and they must take responsibility to seek help themselves to fix these problems. When confronted with a broken partner your job is not to fix them; your job is to leave them and protect your own emotional health.

> **TRAP:** There are many devious men who can sniff and sift women that are natural nurturers. They prey on these women, by telling them, up front; they are broken or emotionally wounded, due to events in their life. They

try to convince them that they just need the love of a good woman, who will turn their fortunes around. Many nurturing women are tenderhearted, with gullible minds, and fall for these shysters, who will do nothing but bring the terrible twins (trauma and drama) into their lives.

SLEEPING BEAUTY COMPLEX

Sleeping Beauty is a fairy tale, which tells the story of a princess, who was cursed, by a witch, to die on her sixteenth birthday. The curse was overturned by a fairy, and rather than die, she would go into a deep sleep and remain that way until a man with a pure heart falls in love with her, and that love will bring her back to life. When Prince Charming finally comes along and kisses her, she awakens and says, "Oh, you have come at last; I was waiting for you in my dream. I've waited so long."

Many women have been conditioned to wait for Prince Charming to come by on his white horse, in shining armor, grab you by the waist, put you on the back of his horse, ride off into the sunset, and live happily ever after. Well my successful, sassy friend, you may have been born at night, but I hope it wasn't last night. If you still believe in fairy tales, there is a reason why you are home alone on weekend nights watching reruns of *Sex in the City*. This does not mean that the right partner isn't out there for you, because they are. It means that many women have unrealistic expectations of what the right partner should be like, and what the relationship should be like.

Some women enter into relationships with high hopes and expectations, and they never get fulfilled, because they are unrealistic. Sometimes the glasses you view the world through are so rose-colored, it distorts reality; and you are left frustrated,

223

discouraged, and unsatisfied. Where does fantasy end and reality begin?

Are you waiting to be romantically rescued from your boring and mundane love life by a Prince? Who is Prince Charming to you? Is it the Denzel Washington, David Beckham, or Derek Jeter-type, who is rich, handsome, and famous? For some women, Prince Charming is the idealized, flawless, romanticized male, who will sweep you off your feet, solve all your problems, pay all your bills, and focus all of their time and attention on you.

Some successful, sassy women are searching for that perfect partner, even though intellectually, rationally, and realistically, they know this person or persona does not exist.

Despite rhyme and reason, women with the Sleeping Beauty complex still believe they will somehow, somewhere find this mystical, mythical, and magical figure. This mind-set sets women up to fail, when it comes to finding the right man and having the relationship she desires and deserves.

Women with the Sleeping Beauty complex often fall in love with love. They refuse to admit that the relationship is not working. They ignore or accept a partner's bad behavior, because they don't want to believe their partner isn't the Prince Charming in their personal fairy tale. These women, with this complex, allow reality to take a back seat to fiction and fantasy.

Some successful, sassy women stand firm in their belief that they don't want or need a Prince Charming type, because they are no damsel in distress and don't need to be rescued. They don't want or need a husband, or a significant other, to have a healthy, happy, and fulfilling life. This view may be a little extreme, but it is accurate in the implication that Prince Charming isn't the answer to a woman's unexciting life.

The Sleeping Beauty complex makes a woman often reject a partner, no matter how intelligent, interesting, considerate, engaging, funny, fit, and emotionally available they are. This rejection is justified, because she tells herself, "I know what I want"; but this want or expectation is predicated on finding and capturing a flawless partner, the perfect man.

When you have this complex, you often miss out on truly good partners, who are committed, caring and courageous, and who want to be married or in a long-term relationship. They may not have movie star looks and swag, like Will Smith or Brad Pitt; but face the fact; you are probably not Jada Pinkett or Angelina Jolie.

I am not advocating or telling any woman to settle for second best; but I am saying, don't have your demands, expectations, and requirements so unrealistic that nobody is ever going to be good enough to fulfill them. I am not telling you to stop looking for your Prince Charming; but I am asking you to review and reconsider your perception of what you think this person should be. In relationship economics, it states, "If you expect to 'have it all' in life or in romance, you will live in a perpetual state of frustration, disappointment, and disillusionment"; you can't have it all.

If you see yourself having some of the traits of Sleeping Beauty, you may want to ask yourself if you have a commitment phobia.

You may not have put a name to it, but your behavior and actions might reflect that you are afraid of commitment. How did you get this way? Maybe you can trace it back to something in your childhood. Perhaps you were a victim of abuse, a child of divorce, had abandonment issues, or dealt with the death of a loved one. Maybe you have been cheated on or manipulated by a conniving partner, who has made you afraid to get close to someone else; some successful, sassy women have chosen their careers over long-term relationships and marriage.

Here are 15 signs that indicate you have a commitment phobia:

1. You are overly critical of your partner and the relationship.

2. You purposely annoy or hurt your partner, to sabotage the relationship.

3. Your partner requirements are unrealistic.

4. You are attracted to partners who are unavailable.

5. You know the relationship is not going anywhere, but you stay anyway.

6. You choose your career over relationships.

7. You are constantly being visited by the terrible twins (trauma and drama).

8. You tend to limit the amount of time you spend with your partner, and you treat them as a low priority.

9. You avoid events or outings that may include your partner's family or friends.

10. You hate planning ahead, because that means commitments.

11. You are often unfaithful in relationships.

12. You can't make the decision to give totally to the relationship, but you can't walk away either.

13. You are a serial dater; and if you get in relationships, they don't last long.

14. You don't like structure, particularly in your personal life.

15. You like the thrill of being chased, but don't like the results of being captured.

TIP: If looking at these signals has convinced you that you have a commitment phobia, don't get discouraged and frustrated; nobody is perfect. Identify which signals represent your behavior, and identify what you need to do to change that behavior. Take responsibility for your life; and by facing your fear, you may have to do things that take you out of your comfort zone; like ending a relationship or not obsessing over a partner. Don't give up or give in to your fear; always believe in yourself.

TRAP: The Sleeping Beauty complex holds every man to the high standard of being so perfect, handsome, and tuned into your every desire and need, that nobody is capable of living up to that expectation. Don't let the Sleeping Beauty complex have you betting your whole romantic life on a dream, a ghost-lover, rather than on someone who is flesh and blood.

HARD-HEARTED HANNAH CONDITION

Hard Hearted Hannah (The Vamp of Savannah) was a popular song in the 1950s; it tells the story of a woman, who was the meanest girl in town. Here are a few of the lyrics that describe her character:

> Who's colder than an Arctic storm,
> Got a heart just like a stone,
> Even ice men leave her alone!

> They call her Hard Hearted Hannah,
> The vamp of Savannah,
> The meanest gal in town;
> Leather is tough, but Hannah's heart is tougher,
> She's a gal who loves to see men suffer!
> To tease 'em, and thrill 'em, to torture and kill 'em,
> Is her delight, they say,
> I saw her at the seashore with a great big pan,
> There was Hannah pouring water on a drowning man!

> Talk of your cold, refrigeratin' mamas,
> Brother; she's a polar bear's pajamas!
> To tease 'em, and thrill 'em, to torture and kill 'em,
> Is her delight, they say,
> An evening spent with Hannah sittin' on your knees,
> Is like travelin' through Alaska in your BVDs.

The Hard-Hearted Hannah condition is a woman who is holding onto a hurt until it has a hold on her; and the hurt has turned her into a cold, heartless, unhappy person, who is swimming in a sea of negative emotions. At the core and center of all of Hard-Hearted Hannah's relationship problems lie strong and overwhelming emotions, such as fear, low self-esteem, unpleasant emotions, such as jealousy, feeling abandoned, feeling hurt, feeling unlovable, feeling trapped, feeling desperate, feeling unloved. These feelings could have many causes.

Here are some possible causes and the negative emotions they illicit:

1. I am tired of him cheating on me (**anger**).

2. I can't stand the thought of him touching me (**repulsion**).

3. I've done so much for him, and he doesn't even know that I exist (**sadness**).

4. I'm sure he's having an affair (**fear, terror, panic**).

5. I don't trust him anymore (**resentment**).

6. That relationship robbed me of my will to live (**depression, sadness, fear**).

7. Nobody will ever love me (**low self-esteem**).

8. I'm not good enough to be loved (**feeling unlovable**).

9. I will never get out of this toxic relationship (**feeling trapped**).

10. He left me for that younger woman (**feeling abandoned**).

11. He told me I was fat and nobody will ever want me (**hurt**).

12. He took his mistress to Las Vegas; he never took me anywhere (**jealousy**).

13. Since he left, I don't know how I can pay my bills (**feeling desperate**).

Whatever causes this Hard-Hearted Hannah condition is rooted in bitterness and resentment, which grows out of the pain of losing something or someone.

Hard-Hearted Hannah blames other people or external situations for having caused her loss, and for her past lover's taking advantage of her unfairly. The blame often only resides in her head and is a product of her imagination. She fails to see things from other people's perspectives. She becomes deeply selfish.

When Hard-Hearted Hannahs are hurt or let down by others, they allow that hurt and disappointment to germinate in their heart, and the hostility and hatred begins to grow.

Hard-Hearted Hannahs are described as having unforgiving spirits and, generally, negative and hypercritical attitudes. Bitterness and resentment pervade every facet of her life and make every day that ends with the letter "y" miserable. If the Hannahs of the world continue to harbor sinful feelings, those same feelings could have physical consequences, such as headaches, ulcers, sleeplessness, heart attacks, anxiety, fear, tension, and depression.

This condition slowly destroys one's peace of mind. It is like emotional suicide.

Hard-Hearted Hannah records every offense that was committed against her. She is always ready to show others how much she has been hurt. She defends her grudges constantly. She feels she has been hurt severely and often; and this excuses her from the need to forgive, or take responsibility for her part in the unsuccessful relationships. The sad thing about Hard-Hearted Hannah is, her heart is so full of resentment and bitterness, that she no longer has the desire or capability to love.

This condition is often the result of events, circumstances, and situations. Hannah is still responsible for what she does, what she says, what she thinks, and what she feels. Nobody can make her bitter; she chooses to respond to situations in a bitter way. Hannah can get rid of all her bitterness, resentment, rage, anger, along with every form of malice, if she wishes to do so. What makes her bitter is her attitude toward people, circumstances, and life.

> **TIP:** When you focus on the thing you don't want, and energize it, by complaining about it passionately, and repeating it to as many people as will listen, this creates a downward spiral of anger. What you focus on expands. Being aware of how much influence your emotions have over your life is the first step to taking charge of them. Your life and circumstances often mirror your thoughts. It is never too late to change your attitude and your life.

Watch your thoughts, they become words.
Watch your words, they become actions.
Watch your actions, they become habits.
Watch your habits, they become your character.
Watch your character, it becomes your destiny.

TRAP: Negative thoughts and emotions are the enemies of having a successful relationship or a victorious life; both are very much determined by your mind and your thoughts. Negative thoughts and emotions distract your focus from the important and drain your energy. Knowing how to overcome negative thoughts and emotions may make the difference between victory and defeat in your life; if you don't overcome these emotional demons, they will rob you of the ingredients necessary for success, happiness, and the chance at a lasting, loving relationship and life.

CHAPTER TEN
RISKY BUSINESS

OPPORTUNIST=ENTREPRENEUR

The decision to start a business, or start a relationship, should not be made blindly. Not everyone is equipped with the necessary skill sets, core competencies, and experiences to successfully start their own business. Some people need the structure and the security that working for a company provides.

Many contemporary women are looking for different opportunities to impact their lives positively. Mr. Webster, in his dictionary, describes an opportunity as a condition favorable for attainment of a goal, with a good chance for success. Modern-day women are setting new goals in their personal and professional lives and recognizing that they need to be more opportunistic. Successful and sassy women want to change their financial and social statuses, because the status quo is no longer acceptable. Their desire for gain outweighs their fear of loss, and they are willing to step out of their comfort zones and do things they have never done before.

In today's global economy, there is a new kind of opportunist and they are called **entrepreneurs.** An entrepreneur is defined as one who organizes, manages, and assumes the **risk** of the success or failure of a business venture. Entrepreneurship is a mind-set for generating an income on your own.

Entrepreneurs come in all sizes, ages, creeds and color. People can discover their entrepreneurial skills either early or late in life. Because of society's antiquated thoughts that women should stay home, barefoot and pregnant, women were not encouraged to become entrepreneurs.

Today, women as a group, and many as individuals, have become economic powerhouses. Women have become the dominant force in small business ownership, succeeding in industries that were once off limits to them. Women own 10.4 million businesses, which means that for every five businesses in this country, two are women-owned. This generates $2.4 trillion for the U.S. economy, and women-owned companies also employ 12.8 million people nationwide.

By nature, most women are not risk takers. They prefer the security of knowing how much they will have each week or month in their paycheck. Many women were not taught to follow their dream or think like an owner; they were conditioned to think as an employee— get a job, keep that job, and retire in that job.

In America, we have become slaves to our job, our creature comforts, our credit cards, and our unhappy relationships. How do we break the chains of bondage and start a new path? One way is for you to begin to take risk. How long have you thought about opening a business? How long have you wanted to end a dead-end relationship? How long have you admired other people for their courage to quit their job and be their own boss?

How many times have you said you were going to get into shape and find you a new man? Now is the time, ladies, to take control of your destiny, your future.

GREAT TRAITS

Love may come naturally, but relationships take work. Any time two individuals find each other, accept each other, and love each other, work is required. A relationship, regardless of how wonderful you both are, is not self-maintaining; and without the necessary care, consideration, and commitment (that is what work is), it will die.

Running a business, or being in a relationship, takes not only work, but also skills. It is the lack of skills that causes many businesses and relationships to fail.

When adversity and tough times visit the workplace or the relationship and work is required to save the business or the romance, does either partner have the requisite skills needed to do the work required?

Why does one successful, sassy, single woman take advantage of a personal or professional opportunity, while another equally successful, sassy, and single woman does not? Is it in their genetic makeup, or does one have special deoxyribonucleic acid (DNA)? I think the difference is in their traits.

I believe the skills and traits it takes to start, run, and grow a business are some of the same skills and traits needed to find, attract, and keep the right man.

Here are the entrepreneurial mind-sets and traits that I believe will help you successfully run a business. They will also help you successfully find a quality partner and have the relationship you desire and deserve.

I have put these traits into four categories:

- Personal characteristics
- Interpersonal skills
- Critical and creative thinking skills
- Practical skills.

I.   Personal Characteristics

Your whole life is affected, both positively and negatively, by the personal characteristics that make you who you are.

- **B-Positive**: This is not a blood type; it's a major mind-set of a successful entrepreneur. Are you a positive thinker? Optimism is truly an asset, and it will help get you through the tough times that many entrepreneurs experience as they find a business model that works for them. A positive attitude is attractive; and men gravitate to a woman, who not only sees the glass full, but also will bring it to him with his favorite liquid refreshment in it. If you want to give your romantic life a transfusion, make it B-positive.

- **Insight:** Can you easily see where things can be improved? Insight is the power of acute observation and deduction, penetration, discernment, and perception. Insight allows you to quickly grasp the "big picture," and explain it to others?

With insight, you can understand the cause and effect of why past relations didn't succeed, based on identification of certain attitudes and actions. Many women have poor insight into their relationship struggles.

- **Initiative**: Initiative is doing what needs to be done, without waiting to be told. Do you take the initiative and instinctively start problem-solving? Can you look across a crowded room, see a man you are attracted to, walk up to him, and introduce yourself? If you want things in your romantic life that you have never had, then you are going to have to take the initiative and start doing things you have never done.

- **Drive and perseverance**: Are you self-motivated and energetic? Are you prepared to work hard and smart, for a very long time, to realize your personal and professional goals? Can you keep going, even if it seems that every date is worse than the one before? Even though your best friends are married or in serious relationships, will you continue to try to find the right man? Quitters never win, and winners never quit.

- **Risk taker**: Are you afraid to fail? Are you afraid of failure? Can you make decisions when the facts are uncertain? Will you go out on a blind date, or spend time with your friend's cousin Vinnie from Jersey? Don't knock it; I met my ex-wife on a blind date.

- **Flexible**: Can you shift gears and move into Plan B mode when things don't go as originally planned? Do you learn and grow from your mistakes and failures? Men like a woman who can roll with the punches or make the best of a bad situation. If you can be at your best when the situation is at its worse, the right man will see that as a virtuous quality. Stars shine in the dark of the night.

II. **Interpersonal Skills**
    In business and romance, you will have to work closely with people. Great relationships are usually formed because of a person's people skills and ability to get along with others.

- **Selling skills**: Are you good at expressing yourself? In both business and romance, selling skills have become more important and more relevant than ever before. We live in a world that is filled with competition. There are so many businesses fighting for the same dollar; and so many single women fighting for the same type of man. In order to rise above the competition, you have to sell your personal features and benefits. They say nothing happens in life until somebody sells something to someone.

- **Communication skills:** Are you competent with all types of communication? You need to be able to communicate well to sell your vision of the future. In business, and relationships, you use language to communicate, to express yourself, to get your ideas across, and to connect with your customer/**partner**. When a relationship is working, the act of communicating seems to flow relatively effortlessly. When a relationship is deteriorating, the act of communicating can be frustrating. A major cause of failed relationships is poor communication.

- **Listening:** Do you hear what others are telling you? Your ability to listen can make or break you as an entrepreneur. Active listeners hear the speaker's content and intent. A woman who knows how to listen to her partner's feedback, comments, and questions is positioned to have relationship success.

- **Negotiating skills:** Negotiation is a vital part of your personal and professional life; you need to be able to resolve differences between people in a positive, mutually beneficial way. Negotiation skills include being well-prepared, showing patience, breaking down bigger issues into smaller ones, avoiding threats and manipulative tactics, focusing on fixing the problem not the blame, and trying to create win-win situations.

- **Ethics:** Do you deal with people based on respect and integrity? You'll find it hard to build a happy, committed relationship at home or at work, if you don't treat people with fairness and truthfulness

- **Good instincts:** Can you read people? You must have an ability to sense what or who is right or wrong. Good instincts help discern when you are being told the truth or lied to. Have you ever had a friend who was dating someone who was just flat out wrong for them, and it made you question what they were thinking about? Chances are your friend has poor instincts and never has developed a BS detector. Knowing whom to get into bed with, literally and figuratively, can be a matter of life and death.

III. **Creative Thinking Skills**

As an entrepreneur, you need to have fresh ideas, and make good decisions about opportunities and potential projects. Many people think that you're either born creative or you're not. Creative thinkers are made, not born.

- **Critical thinking**: Are you able to see situations from a variety of perspectives and come up with original ideas? You must be able to think logically and rationally, to assess data and information and make sense out of it. In business, you are often given incomplete information, but you still have to make decisions.

  By being a critical thinker, you can often make intelligent assumptions and deduce an appropriate answer or solution. Knowing what it's going to take to elevate your relationship to another level often requires both critical and creative thinking.

- **Problem solving**: How good are you at coming up with sound solutions to the problems you're facing? Can you think outside the box; or are you locked in to the conventional way of doing things?

- **Recognizing opportunities:** Do you recognize opportunities when they present themselves? Can you spot a business trend? Are you able to create a plan to take advantage of the opportunities you identify? Knowing when a man is interested and responding appropriately is recognizing an opportunity. Recognizing an opportunity is only an effective skill if it is combined with action.

- **Decision making:** Entrepreneurs, from Day 1, are making decisions about; marketing, funding, production, operations, and customer service. In romance, deciding whom to date is a critical decision. Because your life-mate will be someone you date; deciding on the right partner is a big decision.

- **Strategic planning**: Building effective plans that allow you to achieve current and future goals will guide your business and help determine and define who and what your business is. *The Right Man Business Plan* is an instrument that will help you achieve your relationship goals.

- **Attention to detail**: Can you look at something and immediately see what is out of place or not in order? This is the ability to see patterns, listen, observe, and focus. What if you noticed that your male friend always left your house at the same time? Would it send up a red flag in your mind, like maybe he's seeing someone else, or his other lady friend gets off at that time? Don't judge a person by what they say, judge them by what they do. Paying attention to the small things can prevent big problems.

IV.   Practical Skills

Practical skills are the skills and knowledge that are related to specific useful competencies that help achieve an end result.

- **Goal setting:** Do you regularly set goals, create a plan to achieve them, and then carry out that plan? Without setting goals, how do you know when you have hit your target? Knowing what type of partner and relationship you want helps guide your actions on what to do to get it.

- **Organizing:** Do you have the talents, skills, and abilities necessary to achieve your goals? Can you coordinate people to achieve these efficiently and effectively? A man appreciates a woman, who has organized thoughts and seems to have her life in order and her priorities aligned with the important things in life.

- **Self-management**: The most difficult thing to manage in business is yourself. Being responsible for your actions, staying healthy physically, emotionally, spiritually, and financially goes a long way in finding the right man. Equals attract. It's hard to keep a business or a relationship straight, when you can't keep yourself straight.

- **Knowledge:** You need to have knowledge in several areas when starting or running a business, or being in a romantic relationship. For instance:

- **Business knowledge:** Do you have a good general knowledge of the main functional areas of a business (sales, marketing, finance, and operations), and are you able to operate or manage others in these areas, with a reasonable degree of competence?

- **Entrepreneurial knowledge:** Do you understand how entrepreneurs raise capital? Moreover, do you understand the sheer amount of experimentation and hard work that may be needed to find a business model that works for you?

- **Opportunity-specific knowledge:** Do you understand the market you're attempting to enter, and do you know what you need to do to bring your product or service to market?

- **Venture-specific knowledge:** Do you know what you need to do to make this type of business successful? In addition, do you understand the specifics of the business that you want to start? (This is where it's often useful to work for a short time in a similar business.)

- **Romantic knowledge:** Do you understand the dynamics of friendships, relationships, dating, cohabitation, and marriage?

LET'S GET THIS BUSINESS STARTED

I started my own business, because I was personally frustrated working with, and for, people who had limited vision and were intimidated by my ambition and desire to achieve. After 25 years of working for someone else, I made the decision to start my own business, be my own boss, and walk the financial high wire without a net. My decision was made even more difficult, because I had just divorced, after twenty three years of marriage, and I was faced with alimony and child support payments.

Despite the obstacles, I was determined to make my new venture work. My intention was to start a marketing company, named The Brand Enhancing Strategy Team, (B.E.S.T.). After years of working for other successful companies, I felt I knew what it took to properly position and profitably grow a brand. To show you how sometimes the best-laid plans can go in a different direction; I received an unexpected phone call from a friend and former colleague at Nike, who had left the company, heard I had done the same, and asked if my company did diversity training. One of my positions at Nike was Director of Corporate Diversity, a department that I created for the global giant.

Having worked 3 months developing marketing programs for my new business, it took me all of three minutes to say, "Of course I do diversity training." With that I was hired to conduct diversity training for my first client. This changed my company focus from marketing to training and development. Funny what one phone call can do to change your entrepreneurial direction; God does work in mysterious ways.

As a business owner, I am acutely aware of the risks that come along when you leave the world of wages and become your own boss. When people come to me and say they want to start their own business I ask them one all-encompassing question, "How long can you go without a paycheck?"

To put yourself at risk, you have to want something very much. You must have courage, confidence, and conviction, to commit to the task; so that when difficult times appear and adversity rears its ugly head, you can, and will, persevere. Even though there are other motives that make people take risks, commitment of the heart is the one that will sustain you, because risk-taking is predicated on what you value and on what you love.

The reasons why people start their own businesses are varied and oftentimes personal. It could be an external event that ignited the entrepreneurial fires, like being terminated or downsized from a current job; or a more traumatic event. like a divorce or death of a spouse.

Here are some personal and practical reasons why people go into business for themselves:

5 Personal Reasons	5 Practical Reasons
Get emotional gratification	Get rich
Be your own boss	Prepare for retirement
Have flexible working hours	Supplement income
Stop taking orders	Use business as a tax shelter
Balance work life	Relieve boredom

MAKING THE RIGHT CHOICE

Choosing the right business to start, or choosing the right partner in a relationship, are both critical decisions. Many people choose their business, or their partner, by chance, convenience, or coincidence. Some get lucky and succeed. For every "good luck" success story, there are scores of disillusioned people, who have gone broke financially, by choosing the wrong business; or ended up with a broken heart, by choosing the wrong partner. Too often, people choose a particular business or a particular partner that's right for someone else, but totally wrong for them.

A story: Ursula was a successful print and runway model in her early twenties. Now 43 years old, she wants to open up her own modeling agency. She guided her daughter's modeling career, which included her working fashion shows in Paris, Milan, Tokyo, and New York. Ursula is passionate about the modeling profession and believes her eye for talent and industry contacts will give her a great chance for success.

She wants her agency to focus on fitness, specializing in swimsuit and healthy lifestyle. Confident in her modeling knowledge, Ursula is nervous about her lack of business acumen. Consequently, she is contemplating bringing in a business partner who has experience in running an agency.

There are four basic criteria to use in choosing the right business for you:

1. **The business should be a good match with your personality and interests**. The first Law of Money is to do what you love; the money will come, if you follow your heart. Ursula's knowledge, experience, and love of modeling should be instrumental in building a profitable modeling agency.

2. **Choose a business that has market and profit potential equal to or greater than your financial expectations.** Having a business fail is certainly disappointing; but having your business succeed, only to discover there are no significant monetary rewards, is even more disappointing. Ursula is well aware of the financial potential of a thriving modeling agency.

3. **Choose a business that fills a very specific market niche.** The more narrowly defined the market niche, the easier the marketing of the product/service will be.

   Ursula knew the modeling industry well enough to know there was opportunity in fitness, because other agencies were not focusing on it.

4. **If you want to choose a business that you have interest but no experience in, find a business partner who has the needed experience.** Find a partner who either has the knowledge/experience you don't have, or who agrees to hire a manager who has the needed experience. Ursula is interested in finding a partner who has had experience in running a modeling agency.

History has given us examples of successful partnerships such as Baskin & Robbins, Ben & Jerry, Bill Gates & Paul Allen, Ashford & Simpson, as well as some not so successful partnerships, like Bonnie & Clyde and Thelma & Louise.

In both a business partnership and a romantic partnership, you have to know yourself as well as know your partner, for the partnership to succeed. A good partner must share your vision, passion, and enthusiasm for the business or the relationship.

In business, you want a partner who brings experience and expertise in areas in which you are inexperienced, and someone who understands the legal, financial, and psychological responsibilities germane to sharing a business.

In a romance, you want a partner who is compatible, caring, and considerate of your needs, and who is willing to work with you to make the relationship healthy and successful.

The key to choosing the right business, or romantic, partner, is selecting someone you genuinely like, are compatible with, can communicate with, and have faith in.

A business partnership is like a marriage; both requiring high levels of trust, honesty, and respect. Like marriages, there are unpleasant and expensive divorces in business partnerships, also.

Though you may be madly in love with your partner; before you decide on hopping the broom, you might want to take more time to decide if you are truly compatible. Before choosing a business partner, you might want to "date" first. This means engage in some joint projects, work on a bid together, or do some cross marketing to better gauge how comfortable you are working together.

Before choosing a business partner, or a romantic partner, it is important to take a candid snapshot of your strengths, shortfalls, and skills. Knowing where you might need help and what skills, experiences, and qualities will best complement you, will help in your selection process. It is also critical that you thoroughly evaluate a potential partner's skills, capabilities, personality, and track record. The best indicator of someone's future performance is their past performance. Most successful partnerships/**relationships** are found on complementary skill sets, common goals, and a shared vision.

Something that has always puzzled me is how we use different standards of choosing business partners than we do for relationship partners.

Most women would not choose a business partner who lies, cheats, or is addicted to drugs or alcohol; rationalizing that they could not be trusted with their money. Yet some of these same women will choose a relationship partner who lies, cheats, and is addicted to drugs or alcohol. Is not your heart just as valuable and precious as your money?

I believe you can successfully use the same discernment and decision-making criteria in choosing a business partner as you would a relationship partner.

Here are seven essential things your business, or romantic, partner must have:

1. **Similar values and ethics.** It is critical that your partner be ethically aligned with you and share the same values. In business, they need to be on the same page with you on how the company is set up, what products/services are to be offered, the customer base, the sales approach, the way the financial books are handled, how taxes will be filed, and how each partner will be compensated. In a romance, your partner should have compatible ideas about the five key things that affect relationships: 1) Sex; 2) Money; 3) Family; 4) Religion; and 5)

Communications. Not being in synch with any one of these, could be a stumbling block for a loving and lasting relationship.

2. **Financially stable.** Your partner should know how to manage their own resources and finances; if they can't effectively handle their own finances, chances are they won't handle yours effectively either. Having a business partner who isn't financially stable could potentially present problems in the business, like using company funds to pay personal bills. In romance, a partner with financial problems is always going to be challenging; either you have to pay for everything, or maybe you begin to question his motive in being in the relationship. There are legitimate reasons why a person could be struggling financially, but that doesn't alter the fact that they are a risky and potentially bad choice for a partner.

3. **Able to compromise.** A partner must be willing and able to listen and understand your point of view and perspective on certain topics and situations. Agreeing to disagree, agreeably, helps each side express ideas and opinions without fear of resentment or retaliation. A partner sometimes must swallow their personal pride and focus on what's best for the business or the relationship. A person who knows how to create win-win scenarios, so both parties walk away feeling satisfied, understands the importance of harmony and the role it plays in quality relationships. Sometimes it is better to be happy than right.

4. **Ability to get along with others.** A partner, who likes people and knows how to get along with them, is usually someone who will be an asset to the business or the relationship. In business, a partner who can't get along with people runs the risk of jeopardizing relationships with investors, customers, employees, and suppliers. In a romance, a person who has a bad rapport with his family, or doesn't have many friends, is not a good partner candidate. This statement I am going to make reflects a very strong feeling I have developed over the years. I have used it with my daughters, and I have not seen it proved wrong yet. Here it goes. A man who has a poor relationship with his mother or speaks negatively about her in any form or fashion, will never be able to love you and give you the relationship you want and deserve. I have taken into account that there are probably mothers out there who have earned the disdain of their son, for what they may have done or not done. A man, who refuses to speak with or have a relationship with his mother, doesn't respect the sanctity of "motherhood" and is incapable of loving you in a healthy way. Not only do I strongly advise against beginning a relationship with this person, but if you have found out that this is the case, since you have been in the relationship, I recommend that you leave now, cut your losses, pack up, and move on. If you stay in the relationship, knowing his feelings toward his mother, you will have a long visit from the terrible twins (trauma and drama).

5. **Capacity to work hard and smart.** The only place success comes before work is in the dictionary. Your partner must have a good work ethic, and appreciate the value and need for working both smart and hard. You want a business partner who will come in early and stay late, when needed to get the job done; you want a partner who not only has financial equity in the business but also sweat equity. Romantic relationships, in order to be successful, take work. You want someone who recognizes the need to work consistently on the things necessary to make the relationship thrive—like communication, showing affection, listening, being non-judgmental, and making sure needs are being met. A lazy or unenthusiastic person will be a lazy or unenthusiastic partner. Love is a lifetime of work.

6. **An effective communicator.** The ability to express your feelings, share ideas, and listen to others' cares and concerns is paving a smooth road to relationship and partnership success. The person who can articulate how they feel and what they think eliminates their partner not knowing or understanding how and what they feel or think. The lack of communication is one of the No. 1 reasons why personal and professional relationships are unsuccessful. A person who is comfortable discussing difficult topics, like insufficient funds in the company checking account, or why your ex-wife keeps calling you, is going to be able to resolve conflict and build consensus on most issues.

7. **Commitment to excellence.** You want a partner who won't settle for second best, and is always striving to get better in everything they say and do. Your partner is an extension of yourself, so you want someone who knows what quality is and will not compromise or cut corners to settle for something mediocre or average. You want someone who appreciates the fact that everything the company does is putting the company's reputation on the line. Therefore, everything, from the stationery, to the way the phone is answered, to the way the product/service is delivered, must be top-notch. You want a partner who believes it's either first class or no class. You want a romantic partner to comprehend that perfection is both a journey and a destination, which may never be realized but always pursued. A man who wants the best for his woman, and will not settle for less than the best, is a keeper and someone with whom you may want to have a future.

OPTIONS TO START A BUSINESS

A story: Tonya, a 32-year-old, former professional cheerleader, recently got engaged to a major league baseball player. She made an agreement with Tony, her fiancée, that she would quit cheerleading if he would finance a business for her. Tonya has a marketing degree, but has never used it professionally. She did help organize and market a cheerleader calendar for a local charity, which was very successful and whetted her appetite to start a business. She is confused on what business to start.

She has met with a business consultant, who has suggested a few possibilities and introduced her to three business owners, so she could hear their perspectives and ask questions. Tonya's passion is fashion, and her favorite pastime is shopping; so she believes maybe she should go into retail, possibly a high-end boutique. Tony is pressuring her to do something quick before his season starts.

For Tonya, starting a business is a major decision; it's a big step, and she knows she has a tremendous amount of learning and preparation ahead. There's no question that owning your own business is a risky proposition; but with risk comes reward. Tonya has options she can take concerning starting her own business. These options are:

1. **She can buy a franchise business.** Buying a franchise would allow Tonya to be part of a nationally recognized brand, which already has a successful and proven format that could give expert advice on location, design, capitalization, operation, and marketing.

    The franchisor, in some instances, may provide direct financial assistance. The largest percentage of franchise operations deals with car dealerships, gasoline stations, auto products, and fast food. If Tonya decides to buy a franchise, she needs to assess the success, reputation, and image of the franchising company, visit other franchises, and talk with the Better Business Bureau and the Chamber of Commerce, to investigate the company's track record.

2. **She can buy an existing business.** If Tonya buys an existing business, she would avoid the lead time associated with starting her own business, she would have an active and loyal customer base, have a good idea of what sort of income and expenses to expect, an established building and location, employees who already know the business, inventory/supplies, and a tax and credit history. If Tonya wants to buy an existing business, three critical questions need to be asked: 1) is the asking price fair market value for the business? 2) for the same money, would you be better off building your own business image and acquiring new equipment or a different location? and 3) how long would it take to build the same customer base if you started the business from scratch? Before she would sign on the dotted line, she needs to consult with an attorney, a CPA, a banker, current employees, the Better Business Bureau, and Dun & Bradstreet (the world's leading source of commercial information and insight on businesses).

3. **She can create a licensing agreement.** Licensing would be a viable option for Tonya, if she has a product or a product idea that she wants to mass-market, but doesn't want to assume the risk and responsibility of manufacturing and distributing the product. Under a licensing agreement, she would grant another party (the licensee) the right to produce and market the product.

In exchange for granting this right, Tonya would receive a percentage of income (a royalty) from the sale of the licensed product. Another situation in which licensing might work for Tonya is if she wants to manufacture and or distribute her product herself but wants to have a trademark logo. If she created a product that she wanted to market with the Major League Baseball (MLB) logo, she could enter into a license agreement with the licensing arm of MLB, to use their logo on her product. In exchange for this right, Tonya would pay MLB (the licensor) a royalty on income generated from the sale of her product. This agreement may greatly increase market penetration by giving her product instant name recognition, access to an existing sales force, participation in trade shows, and discount advertising rates. Tonya should be aware that others may try to imitate or steal her ideas. If she licenses another party to produce and distribute her product, she must protect the intellectual property rights associated with the product, such as patent, copyright and trademark rights.

4. **She can start a business from scratch.** Starting fresh with a new business certainly gives Tonya the most freedom, since she is not restricted by what has gone before, not regulated by someone else's rules. She can choose the name, pick the location, hire the employees, define the company's personality, and have the satisfaction of knowing that she did it herself.

In many cases, starting from scratch is the lowest-cost approach to starting a business. The success of most start-up businesses rests upon the ability to raise capital; Tonya has this covered because of her fiancée's offer to fund the business. No two businesses are the same; each has its own requirements, but generally they are either "capital-intensive," requiring a great deal of money to start up, or they are "labor-intensive," requiring more people than equipment to start up.

If Tonya is going to start her business from scratch, she should be aware of:

- Start-up cost
- Fixed cost (business expenses that are not dependent on the level of goods or services produced by the business) and variable cost (expenses that change in proportion to the activity of the business)
- Profit and loss projections for the first year
- Projected cash flow
- Year-end net worth
- Where to locate the business
- Deciding on the legal form for the company.

There must be some reason why some 600,000 new businesses are founded each year. Starting your own business can allow you to control your own professional and financial destiny; while providing a work/life balance that fits the life and lifestyle you want to live.

Running a business is a 24/7 process. Finding the right man can also be a 24/7 process. In both enterprises, you have to be patient and diligent. You cannot expect to try something one time and get instant results. I have had clients ask me how long would my training or consulting take to fix their company problem; and I would ask them, how long did it take to get to the state it is in now? What took 6 years to develop, they want me to fix in 6 hours, or in 6 days, or in 6 months. I might be good, but I'm no miracle worker.

Please give the things you learn in this book time to be understood, implemented, and evaluated.

The Right Man Business Plan is bringing the future into the present, so that you can do something about it now.

Remember; it wasn't raining when Noah built the Ark.

Answer the following questions:

1. What entrepreneurial traits do you have?

_____

_____

_____

2. Which of these traits would help you in a romantic relationship?

_____

_____

_____

3. What would be the reason you would start your own business?

_____

_____

_____

4. What kind of business would you start?

_____

_____

_____

5. Would you buy a franchise business? Why or why not?

_____

_____

_____

6. Would you buy an existing business? Why or why not?

_____

_____

_____

7. Would you sign a licensing agreement? Why or why not?

_____

_____

_____

8. Would you start your business from scratch? Why or Why not?

_____

_____

_____

9. What would be your biggest barrier in starting a business?

_____

_____

_____

10. Whom would you pick to be your business partner? Why?

_____

_____

_____

CHAPTER ELEVEN
LEARN FROM THE PAST

MISTAKES ARE PART OF LIFE

There are a few things that you will do as long as you keep living; and one of those things is making mistakes. Sometimes, no matter how hard you try, how long you prepare, or how many times you double-check, a mistake occurs. Part of being human means you are imperfect and fallible; human beings are designed to learn more by failing and making mistakes than from their successes. Some people might say mistakes make you stronger and smarter; but I say, "Mistakes will never make you stronger and smarter, if you refuse to learn from them." Underneath every mistake in business or in relationships is a valuable lesson.

Unfortunately, many entrepreneurs and romantic partners miss these lessons. They blame others for the mistakes. I say, accept responsibility and don't blame anyone. When you blame, you give power to someone else; but when you accept responsibility, you will be forced to look into yourself and seek answers. Taking responsibility for the mistake puts you in control.

Failed relationships or failed businesses are part of a learning process; it's what makes the game of romance and entrepreneurship challenging and exciting.

Mistakes are part of the process of building a business and a relationship; they are great learning tools.

If you know why businesses fail, you can avoid making those mistakes.

Here are seven reasons why the majority of businesses fail:

- Lack of cash flow
- Wrong location
- Inadequate marketing plan
- Didn't thoroughly research the competition
- Wrong choice of business
- Business grew too quickly
- No planning and poor management

Mistakes occur in relationships for various reasons. To avoid repeating them, you need to understand the underlying reason why they were made.

The following are three examples of failed relationships. There are things to be learned from each situation, which can help you in reviewing your past relationships and preparing for your future one.

MAYBE I MOVED TOO FAST

A story: Lucy is a 36-year-old author of children's books. She is very successful and is financially able to retire due to a shrewd investment in a dot.com stock. She is a romantic, who feels her biological clock is ticking and is a little jealous of her girlfriends who have partners. She is recovering from a failed relationship with Sean, a 29-year-old firefighter.

The whirlwind relationship started like a house of fire and ended up in flames. When she met Sean, she was lonely and romantically depressed, feeling she would never meet the right man. When she first saw him in the mall, she was immediately attracted, mainly because of his physique. He had broad shoulders, bulging biceps, and a cute behind. He also noticed her, and after six hours in Starbucks talking, listening, and lusting, the dating game began. Three months into the relationship, Lucy noticed that Sean was quite different from her. She was religious, he was agnostic; she was kind and caring, he was cold and aloof; she was about family, he never talked about his family. These differences in values have caused problems between the two. She thought he would change over time and her influence would accelerate his metamorphosis. It was apparent that Lucy really did not know Sean very well, and maybe she should have slowed the pace of the relationship. Despite their satisfying physical relationship, Lucy was unfulfilled in every other area that was important to her. Sean became controlling and abusive, which scared her. Due to Sean's actions and attitude, after she ended the relationship, Lucy was forced to get a restraining order against Sean. To avoid any possible retaliatory acts by Sean, Lucy is contemplating relocating.

If Lucy honestly would evaluate her relationship with Sean, she would see how she made seven classic mistakes that led to her failed relationship.

Here are the seven mistakes she made:

1. She allowed her hormones to make her decisions about Sean. Chemistry is the animal attraction that is purely physical. While chemistry is important, without compatibility as a complimentary component, the prospects of a healthy relationship are very slim. What looks good to you might not always be good for you. **Chemistry should not do your picking of a partner.**

2. Lucy was lonely, and believed she heard her maternal instincts calling her name. Choosing a partner to avoid loneliness, trying to keep up with friends, or wanting to have a baby, are all unhealthy reasons to get involved in a relationship. Even being with Sean, Lucy was still lonely. **Avoiding loneliness is not a reason to be in a relationship**. Getting involved in relationships for misguided purposes is a surefire recipe for a visit from the terrible twins (trauma and drama).

3. **Lucy did not ask enough questions before she got involved with Sean**. You have to know about a person's past behaviors, because they are the best indicators of his future behaviors. Part of the reason for dating is to get to know as much as you can about a person, so you can intelligently decide if you want to be in a relationship with them.

4. **Lucy and Sean did not share the same values,** and this led to conflicts. Lucy wanted a family and Sean never wanted to discuss it. Two people unequally yoked on important matters, like faith, family, and finances, will never be able to have a healthy relationship.

5. **Lucy expected Sean to change**. Most adults are set in their ways and don't like the idea of changing. If Sean was annoying or offensive while they were dating, he was going to be the same way in the relationship. To get into a relationship with a person and expect them to change or conform to your expectation is unreasonable.

6. **Lucy is in love with the idea of love**. Being a romantic often confuses fantasies with relationship realities. Neither Sean nor any other man can live up to the expectations and perceptions of fantasies. Fantasy love inhibits the openness required for two people to see and appreciate the unique qualities of their partner. See the Sleeping Beauty complex.

7. Not knowing Sean as well as she needed to, **Lucy moved too fast,** accelerating the relationship before she knew what and with whom she was getting involved. Understanding the different stages in relationships helps to avoid moving too fast.

HOPE IS NOT A STRATEGY

A story: Dominique, a 42-year-old naturalized U.S. citizen has been widowed for four years. Her husband, whom she met in high school in her native country, the Dominican Republic, died from pancreatic cancer. She works for a large social service agency, where she is a team leader for a group of data entry specialists. Often mistaken for the actress Selma Hayek, Dominique is attractive with a pleasant personality. She was skeptical of getting back into the dating scene, but she has gone out on several blind dates, set up by her girlfriends. Each one has been a disaster, except for Victor. For the first time since her husband's death, she felt connected to someone. He was charming, funny, and respectful; but after seven months, the relationship ended. He told her he was uncomfortable with her inability to share her feelings. He never knew where he stood with her, and he wasn't sure he could wait for her concerning her desire not to be sexual. Dominique's despair over the breakup has caused her to retreat even deeper into her shell. She misses

Victor, wants him back, and hopes the relationship can work; but she doesn't know how or what to do to fix it.

Hope is a wish in your heart for good things to come. Hope happens when someone sees something, decides that it is desirable, realizes that they may not get it, but believes that there is still a chance of getting it.

Casinos and the lotteries are built on hope. People in business and in romance are hoping for things. In business, they are hoping for more customers, more sales, and greater profits. Similarly, in romance, they are hoping for a quality partner and a quality relationship.

There are three types of hope:

- **Desperation.** Desperate hope is when a woman will do almost anything to get or keep her man, even if it violates her values.

- **Optimistic.** Optimistic hope is a positive hope with a very low probability of occurring.

- **Realistic hope.** Realistic hope is based on a fair estimation of probabilities (over 50 percent chance it will occur).

Dominique doesn't appear to be desperate. She knows she's an attractive woman and men will always be available to her. Her husband was her high school sweetheart and the only man she has ever been intimate with sexually. Her religious upbringing makes her feel that sex should only be with her husband. Her friends have made fun of her and told her she doesn't know what she is missing; but her values are important to her, and she will let them be her moral compass. She hopes that if she has a chance to speak with Victor, they would get back together. Though her deceased husband was the only man she has ever loved, she was getting near the love zone with Victor. Does Dominique have a realistic hope of having a successful relationship with Victor, or is she fooling herself?

It is not what Dominique hopes for that matter; what matters is, what is she going to do to make her hope a reality?

Before Dominique attempts to get Victor back, here are four key things she must do:

- She must ask herself if Victor is able to fulfill some of her emotional needs, and if can she fulfill his. A man leaves a relationship for a variety of reasons. Some of those reasons are; he doesn't feel comfortable around you, you have no new things to share with him, he feels he can't learn anything from you, or you aren't contributing to his growth as a human being. If you aren't giving your man some of the above-mentioned things, he will find somebody who will. To win Victor back, Dominique is going to have to make changes, especially in how she communicates.

- She is going to have to make Victor feel important, by sharing with him how she feels about him. She has not really connected with him. If men don't feel important or special, they are not motivated to stay. If you make a man feel he is easily replaceable, he will find someone who makes him feel special. Dominique is going to have to do a better job of connecting with Victor and not hold back expressing her feelings of how she feels about him.
- She has to understand what Victor wants out of life and the relationship. The topic of sex should have been

discussed while they were dating, so that she could have done a better job of managing his expectations. There does not appear to be a lot of fun in this relationship. If a man is growing and getting his needs met in a relationship, why would he want to end it? Dominique and Victor should talk more about what the other wants in the relationship and life.

- Men want to know they are doing a good job in their relationship. Dominique has to assure Victor that he is handling his business quite well in the relationship and he makes her feel respected, cared for, loved, and her emotional needs are being met by him.

WHY DID MY MAN LEAVE?

A story: Freda, 34-year-old corporate lawyer for a Big 5 accounting firm was in a two-year relationship with Stan, one of her co-workers. What started out as friends doing lunch, turned into a full-meal-deal. Freda is arrogant and demanding, which has often led to some heated arguments with Stan. When they first met, Freda was tight, tanned, and toned. Since she was assigned to a new department, which has kept her extremely busy, she has put on weight and let her hair and nail appointments come and go. Stan treats her great while overlooking some of Freda's flaws, he focuses on her strengths; she is smart, creative, and highly sexual, to the point of being overbearing. He has become somewhat uncomfortable with her desire to know his every move and try to control where he goes and what he does with his free time. While Freda has hinted at marriage, Stan has made it clear that it is way too premature for that kind of talk. Stan was previously engaged, but his fiancée was killed in an auto accident three months before the wedding. When planning a vacation to the Hamptons. Freda called Stan to see if they could use his reward miles for the flights; Stan informed her that he was ending the relationship and transferring to another office. Freda, after calling Stan everything but a child of God, and threatening to ruin him is devastated and feeling emotionally unstable.

Are you single because your man left, and you aren't really sure why? You thought things were good, you had fun, and he even introduced you to his friends and family.

Men leave relationships for a variety of reasons. Sometimes, they leave a good relationship for a bad reason, and leave a bad relationship for a good reason. Why do men leave relationships?

When a man leaves a relationship, it doesn't mean it was the woman's fault. Many men enter relationships with issues and baggage, and sometimes not just one or two bags, but a complete set. Some of these issues and baggage that he's carrying around might play a major role in why he leaves a relationship, but some reasons **can** be attributed to the woman or other external factors.

Freda is confused about why Stan left her, but their relationship reveals some of the classic reasons why men leave relationships.

- **Reason 1.** Stan probably had not gotten over his fiancée, when he began the relationship with Freda; and he is comparing his current relationship to his **memories of his past relationship**. Some men hold on to a former girlfriend and put her on a pedestal, which prevents them from appreciating and loving someone else.

  A woman must know her partner has gotten over his past relationship and his former lover, because no woman, no matter how successful and sassy she may be, can win over an idealized memory. Don't let a man who lives in a dream turn your life into a nightmare.

- **Reason 2.** Due to the devastating loss of his previous girlfriend, Stan may have a **fear of commitment** to another person. Some men value their freedom so much that they are not going to relinquish it for any reason, not even love. You need to make sure that your partner isn't fearful of losing his independence or his personal space, and that he is ready mentally and emotionally to have only one sex partner. Do you have similar values and priorities? Here are three questions you must ask yourself, to see if you and your partner could have a future together: **1)** can you communicate honestly; **2)** do you feel safe expressing your deepest fears; and **3)** can you solve problems and resolve issues together? If your partner has dated unavailable women in the past or ended relationships before they were too serious, or has a long list of unrealistic requirements for what he wants in his partner, he is probably fearful of commitment, and you might need to cut your losses.

- **Reason 3.** Most men do not like women who are **demanding, controlling, and stuck on themselves.** Men appreciate and respond favorably to independent women, who are very comfortable in their own skin; they get uncomfortable when a woman tries to control the relationship. Ladies, you must give your man his own space and not smother him by constantly hanging around and being too clingy. Let him miss you and wish you were near him, rather than wondering when are you going to leave. Freda was in some ways all of the above.

- **Reason 4.** Stan was attracted to Freda, because she was physically appealing to him and that excited him. Freda started gaining weight and not keeping herself as well groomed, and Stan may have experienced a **loss of attraction.**

    When a man no longer feels attracted to his mate, then the whole relationship becomes harder and takes more work to try and make it work. Never forget; men are visual, and appearance is important.

Now, some of you might be thinking, how dare that man judge me about my appearance, when he is fat, balding, and out of shape. I agree with you; but as we know, some men have more nerve than a cat burglar.

Here are seven things men want you to do:

- Take care of your health.
- Eat well, exercise regularly.
- Stay active.
- Dress appropriately.
- Be aware of your appearance.
- Have a good attitude.
- Smile and laugh.
- **Reason 5.** There are not many things that make a man leave a relationship more than an **emotionally unstable partner.** Chances are, the way Freda responded when Stan broke up with her was not the first time she revealed glimpses of anger and rage.

271

When a person's emotional stability is in question, many men begin to devise an exit strategy. Despite Freda's intelligence and other good qualities, being an emotional loose cannon, with a hair-trigger temper, does not help in maintaining a healthy relationship. When a partner is unstable emotionally, eventually the two twins (trauma and drama) either visit the relationship or take permanent residency; and sometimes the work it takes to keep the relationship together weighs too heavy on the partner, and he/she leaves.

EVALUATE TO EDUCATE

A part of *The Right Man Business Plan* is an assessment. This is a systematic effort to learn from experience; it enables you to make sense of your past relationship, your impact on it, and its impact on you. The understanding that comes from careful evaluation and honest assessment empowers you to act more effectively and do three critical things:

- Analyze the relationship, and figure out why and what went wrong
- Look for corrective measures to avoid future mistakes
- Implement acquired knowledge in the next relationship.
- If you don't learn from the mistakes of a failed relationship, you will repeat them.

PART ONE – ASSESSMENT

1. Briefly describe your last relationship. (Who ended it, how did it end, etc.?)

_____

_____

2. What worked in the relationship?

_____

_____

3. What didn't work?

_____

_____

4. What did you learn about yourself?

_____

_____

5. What could you have done differently?

_____

_____

6. What will you do differently in your next relationship?

_____

_____

7. What do you think it's like to be in a relationship with you?

_____

_____

8. How would your last partner describe you?

_____

_____

9. When you were dating, did you ignore any red flags about your partner? If so, what were they?

_____

_____

10. Do you have any guilt or regrets?

_____

_____

11. Did you know what you wanted from the relationship? If you didn't receive it, did you share that with your partner?

_____

_____

12. Did you know what your partner wanted?

_____

_____

13. How would you describe the way you and your partner communicated?

_____

_____

14. How much fault are you accepting for the failed relationship?

_____

_____

15. Did the relationship make you bitter or better, and why?

_____

_____

Answer the following questions Yes or No:

1. Did you two share common values? _____

2. Did you feel safe with this person? _____

3. Were you comfortable expressing your feelings? _____

4. Did he treat other people well? _____

5. Was there something about him you wanted to change? _____

6. Do I still have feelings for him? _____

7. Do you see yourself getting back with him? _____

8. Are you a better person after being in this relationship? _____

9. Did you respect and like your partner? _____

10. Do you think this relationship is negatively affecting you? _____

No relationship is a failure, if you leave with a lesson learned; that makes you wiser and better equipped to make the next relationship healthier and more successful.

CHAPTER TWELVE
RELATIONSHIP STRATEGY

WHAT IS YOUR STRATEGY

Today's societal influences and forces have created new behaviors, new opportunities, and new challenges for a woman to find, attract, and keep the right man. To either start a business and manage it successfully, or find a life partner and have a healthy relationship, you need a strategy. Strategy is a long-term plan of action, designed to achieve a particular goal.

The purpose of a business strategy is to exploit the capabilities of your company, in order to gain, sustain, and maintain competitive advantage in meeting and exceeding the needs of your customers.

The purpose of a relationship strategy is to find, attract, and keep a quality partner, who is right for you— and then have a loving, lasting relationship.

A successful, sassy, single woman, who does not have a clear relationship strategy, is like a ship without a rudder. She will not be steady on a particular course; subsequently, she will drift from relationship to relationship.

Following the strategy of this book will provide you with a clear relationship map, consisting of a set of guiding principles and rules. This map will define the actions you need to take, as well as the ones you should not take, to achieve your relationship goals.

Effective strategic planning for a quality relationship begins with an honest and realistic appraisal of the current position or situation you are in; the formal term for this is "situational analysis." To determine your current relationship situation, answer the following questions:

How would you describe where your romantic life is now?

_____

_____

_____

Where do you want your romantic life to be in the next 6-12 months?

_____

_____

_____

What do you think you need to do to get it there?

_____

_____

_____

There are two essential elements in creating your relationship strategy:

- **Vision statement** – the non-specific directional and motivational guidance for your romantic relationship.

- **Goals** – SMART goals that set out what the relationship aims to achieve.

VISION STATEMENT

A story: Yolanda is a 27-year-old, third-year, OB-GYN resident. Her parents met when her dad was stationed in Germany, while in the United States Air Force. Yola, the name her close friends call her, has lived in four countries and six different states. Since she was nine years old, her dream has been to become a doctor, marry a doctor, and raise a child who will be a doctor. At 12, she wrote a school essay declaring that she would graduate from high school at 16, and attend medical school at 21 years old; and that is exactly what has happened. She has dated Malachi for two years, he is a second-year resident at the same hospital. They have already picked a date for their wedding, the city they will both practice in, and the name of their unborn child. Their relationship has had some difficulties, but always survived, mainly because of their shared vision. Yolanda wrote her vision statement on an index card; she keeps it on her or near her at all times, and she reads it daily. She attributes where her life is today, to her faith, focus, and family.

If you do not know where you are going, any road will take you there.

Once you decide where you want to go, or what you want to do personally or professionally, it's easier to determine what roads can take you there. When it comes to having a healthy relationship, you must be a "meaningful specific," not a "wandering generality." Yolanda, at a very young age, knew what she wanted and the roads that would take her there. Just imagine if you were as dialed-in on what you wanted in a partner and a relationship as Yolanda is. It would have saved you from the boring dates, painful relationships, and traumatic breakups.

A relationship vision statement captures your dreams and hopes for your romantic future. It reminds you of what you are trying to build. It should act as an inspiration to you and your future life partner. In summary, it answers the question, "Where do you romantically want to go? The vision statement is your romantic compass.

Here is Yolanda's relationship vision statement: **I have a rewarding relationship with a caring and ethical man, who is a medical doctor, who loves and respects me, by both his words and actions. I look forward, in the next few years, to being married to this man for the rest of my life. I believe this man is my God-delivered partner; and together, we will raise a wonderful child, who will desire to be in the medical profession.**

Yolanda had a dream that is becoming reality right before her eyes. One of the greatest dreamers of our time, and a man I have always admired, was Walt Disney.

Here was a man who created things that the world had never seen before, like the first sound cartoon, the first all-color cartoon, and the first animated feature- length motion picture. He was a lifelong dreamer, who used a four-step process—**Dream,**

Believe, Dare, Do. He explained his success this way: **"I dream, I test my dreams against my beliefs, I dare to take risks, and I execute my vision to make those dreams come through."**

When it comes to you and your relationship quest, you can use the same process that Walt Disney used. Dream about having the partner and the relationship you want; believe it will happen; dare to say no, when saying yes would put you on the wrong road; and do the things needed to make your dream a reality.

Take your time writing what you want in the future, when it comes to your partner and a relationship. Write it in the first person, as if you are already making these things happen in your life.

My personal relationship vision statement

_____

_____

_____

GOALS

A story: Donna prides herself on being organized and goal-oriented. She is disciplined enough to have run the New York Marathon, and is currently training to compete in a triathlon. Not many 37-year-olds have two percent body fat, run five miles every day, and have a healthy relationship. Thomas, a 44-year-old chef, has been Donna's partner for five years. If you looked at what Donna wrote, while she was in college, on the type man she was waiting for, it would be Thomas, to a tee. In great detail, she wrote the following: He will be 6 ft.,2 in., 200 lb., and have a full beard. He will be kind, affectionate, and supportive. He will be an extrovert, with a sense of humor, who has a positive mental outlook. In addition, he will be intelligent, flexible, and a great listener, who likes to give and receive massages, is a good cook, and isn't afraid to make a commitment.

She met Thomas at a friend's party, and they immediately connected, which led to an instant romantic relationship. Donna knew what she was looking for in a partner and when she saw it in Thomas, magic happened.

Many women haven't spent enough time thinking about what they want in a partner, or from a relationship, and haven't set any formal goals. Not many people would set out on a journey without a destination in mind; yet when it comes to relationships, they do it all the time. Donna's process of setting goals helps her choose what she wants out of life. By knowing precisely what she wanted in a partner, Donna knew who and who not to concentrate her efforts.

Goal setting has helped Donna decide what she wanted to achieve in life and in her relationship. It has allowed her to stay focused and not be distracted by irrelevant things. Achieving her goals through goal setting, has helped Donna stay encouraged and built up her self-confidence.

Goal setting is used by top-level athletes, successful businesspeople, and women looking for the right life partner. Setting goals gives you long-term vision and short-term motivation; and meeting your goals is a tremendously rewarding experience. For a relationship to be fruitful and satisfying, you must set clear goals.

Setting goals will help you focus on specific aims over a period of time. Here is a simple acronym used to set goals; it is called SMART. SMART stands for:

- **Significant:** Goals should be impactful and make a positive difference in your life. Here are questions to ask yourself: What am I going to do? Why is this important for me to do? Who else needs to be involved? When do I want this to be completed? How am I going to do this?

- **Measurable:** You should be able to measure whether you are meeting the objectives or not. Measurement is the most important consideration. When will you know that you've achieved your goal? It is also important for feedback purposes.

- **Action-oriented:** Are the goals that you set designed to make positive things happen? Will they produce action?

- **Rewarding:** Once you achieve the goal, will it be something that has positive benefits?

- **Time-bound:** When do you want to achieve the set goals?

Take the time to write out a list of seven things that you want in a relationship, 5 things you want in a partner, and three things you are going to do to ensure that you get both.

5 things you want in a Relationship:

1._____

2._____

3._____

4._____

5._____

5 things you want in a Partner:

1._____

2._____

3._____

4._____

5._____

What goals are you setting to get both the partner and relationship you want:

_____

_____

_____

After you have completed the list, ask yourself why these goals are so important to you at this point in your life. You must understand why you are setting these goals and then decide if you are setting them for the right reasons.

Writing down your goals creates the road map to your relationship success. Although just the act of writing them down can set the process in motion, it is also extremely important to review your goals frequently. Remember, the more focused you are on your goals; the more likely you are to accomplish them.

Every time you make a decision during the day, ask yourself this question, "Does it take me closer to, or further from, my goal." If the answer is "closer to," then you have made the right decision. If the answer is "further from"; well, you know what to do.

By setting sharp, clearly defined goals, you can measure and take pride in the achievement of those goals. You will also raise your self-confidence, as you recognize your own ability and competence in achieving the goals that you have set.

READY, AIM, FIRE

You have completed exercises in this chapter, which have positioned and prepared you to be successful. Whether you were going to start a business or begin a new relationship, you have developed a strategy that will lead you to achieve your goals.

By establishing your vision and creating goals, you have now established a clear road map, defining who you are and what you want out of a relationship and a life partner.

As a successful, sassy, single woman, you must have a strategy to achieve your relationship goals.

CHAPTER THIRTEEN
MARKET PLAN

MARKET SIZE COUNTS

The market analysis is one of the most important components of the market plan. The market analysis provides insight into the structure and size of the market, as well as information concerning the environment that influences the market. It should answer the following questions:

1. What do customers want to buy? How do they want to buy it? When do they want to buy it? What are their preferences, purchasing behavior, and perceptions?

2. Where is the market located?

3. What is the size of the market or the total number of potential customers for your services or products?

4. What are the external factors influencing business activity in this market?

5. What is the average income in your market area? Is your product in alignment with the income, lifestyle, and demographics of your market segment?

6. What is the primary market niche(s) that you plan to serve with your business? What are the current trends influencing this niche?

7. How does the local market compare to the industry as a whole?

8. What do you know about your customers and the marketplace?

9. What strategies do your competitors use to compete in this market?

10. Where is there an opportunity to innovate and compete on a new level?

IDENTIFYING YOUR TARGET MARKET
(ELIGIBLE PARTNERS)

Your target market is simply the market (group of customers) that you want to target (focus on and sell to). When you are defining your target market, it is important to narrow it to a manageable size. Many businesses make the mistake of trying to be everything to everybody. Oftentimes, this philosophy leads to failure. In this section, you should gather information, which identifies the following:

- **Distinguishing characteristics of the major/primary market that you are targeting.** This section might include information about the critical needs of your potential customers, the degree to which those needs are (or are not) currently being met, and the demographics of the group. It would also include the geographic location of your target market, the identification of the major decision-makers, and any seasonal or cyclical trends that may impact the industry or your business.

- **Size of the primary target market**. Here, you would need to know the number of potential customers in your primary market, the number of annual purchases they make in products or services similar to your own, the geographic area they reside in, and the forecasted market growth for this group.

- **The extent to which you feel you will be able to gain market share** and the reasons why. In this research, you would determine the market share percentage and number of customers you expect to obtain in a defined geographic area. You would also outline the logic you used to develop these estimates.

Race/Ethnicity	Number	Percentage of U.S. population
Not Hispanic or Latino	258,267,944	83.7%
White	196,817,552	63.7%
Black or African American	37,685,848	12.2%
Asian	14,465,124	4.7%
Two or more races	5,966,481	1.9%
American Indian or Alaska Native	2,247,098	0.7%
Some other race	604,265	0.2%
Native Hawaiian or other Pacific Islander	481,576	0.2%
Hispanic or Latino	50,477,594	16.3%
White	26,735,713	8.7%
Some other race	18,503,103	6.0%
Two or more races	3,042,592	1.0%
Black or African American	1,243,471	0.4%
American Indian or Alaska Native	685,150	0.2%
Asian	209,128	0.1%
Native Hawaiian or other Pacific Islander	58,437	0.0%
Total	**308,745,538**	**100.0%**

UNDERSTANDING THE MARKET

According to the United States Census Bureau, there are 308.8 million people in the United States and 151.8 million of them are male.

The U.S. population's distribution, by race and ethnicity, in 2010 was as follows:

There are more than 18.1 million American men who are single; of this total, 14.8 million are bachelors, 2.2 are widowers, and 1.1 are divorced. Why do so many men not choose to take a wife? It is not because there are not enough available single women, since unmarried women outnumber unmarried men by 3.4 million. Leading psychologists, sociologists, and other authorities who have researched, studied, and analyzed the dating and mating habits of unmarried men have reached some conclusions about the American bachelor. If a man is still single when he reaches the age of 35, he will probably never marry. Most men who really want to get married find a wife by their late-20s. Most men, whether single, widowed, or divorced, spend a good portion of their time searching for a partner.

The average age for an American male is 35.6 years old. The age segments look like this:

Age Group – Male	Total Population
24-29	10.6 million
30-34	10.0
35-39	10.0
40-44	10.4

45-49	11.2
50-54	10.9
55-59	9.5
60-64	8.0

Median personal income by educational attainment for males 25+ years old

Education	Income
Some H.S	$24,192
H.S. Grad.	$32,085
Some College	$39,150
Associate Degree	$42,382
Bachelor's Degree	$52,265
Bachelor's Degree or Higher	$60,493
Master's Degree	$67,123
Doctorate Degree	$78,324
Professional Degree	$100,000

According to the U.S. Census Bureau, there are 97.2 males for every 100 females in the U.S.A. In general, Western states have the highest male-to-female ratios, while states in the Mid-

Atlantic and Deep South have more women than men. Thirty-nine states have more females than males, while 10 have more males. California is the only state with exactly one male for every female. Illinois exactly matches the national average with 97.2 males for every 100 females.

There are only 89.7 males for every 100 females in the District of Columbia; this is far lower than any full-fledged state. Rhode Island and Maryland both have 93.8 men for every 100 women, the fewest of any states. At the other extreme, Alaska has 108 males for every 100 females, the most of any state. Nevada comes in second with 103.8 males for every 100 females.

WHERE IS THE MARKET?

In a special survey, conducted exclusively for *The Oprah Winfrey Show*, *Men's Health* magazine came up with the 20 best cities in America to meet single men over 35. The results are based on six criteria: the ratio of unmarried men to unmarried women, divorce rates, fitness level, philanthropy, education level, and attraction.

- San Jose, California
- Salt Lake City, Utah
- Arlington, Texas
- Raleigh, North Carolina
- San Francisco, California
- Fremont, California
- Austin, Texas
- Minneapolis, Minnesota
- Washington, D.C.
- San Diego, California
- Charlotte, North Carolina

- Dallas, Texas
- Denver, Colorado
- St. Paul, Minnesota
- Seattle, Washington
- Houston, Texas
- New York, New York
- Madison, Wisconsin
- Fort Worth, Texas
- Durham, North Carolina

KNOWING THE CUSTOMER
(MEN)

The more you know about your customers, the more effective your sales and marketing efforts will be. Customers are the lifeblood of most businesses. Without enough customers, or enough of the right kind of customers, businesses go bad or go broke. It is important that you know what customers consider most valuable about your product. Why does your customer buy? Customers have different motivations when they buy. Some consider price as the main deciding factor, while others find it to be quality.

Most of all, customers buy your product because of the value that it can give them; they are not just buying the product, they are buying what the product can give them. One of the key components in marketing and business growth is to spend time nurturing customer relationships, so that you can get more business. While every business needs to capture new customers, the focus and priority should be on pleasing the existing customer base. Companies that fail to nurture and retain their customer base ultimately fail.

When it comes to customers there are key questions a business owner must ask:

1. **Who** they are
2. **What** they buy
3. **Why** they buy it
4. **How** they use the product
5. **When** they buy
6. **How** they buy
7. **How** much money they have
8. **What** makes them feel good about buying
9. **What** they expect of your business
10. **What** they think of you

The answers to these questions will determine the relationship that you will have with the customer. The essence of good customer service is forming a relationship with the customer and satisfying their needs.

In the world of romance, you— the successful, sassy, single lady—are the product, and products are designed to satisfy the needs of customers; and your customers are single men who are interested in you. The customer (single men) today is more demanding; he has great expectations, and has more choices than ever before when it comes to single females. The internet and online dating are empowerment tools, providing men with a myriad of options that they never had before. In the past, his pool of eligible females was local; and now, due to technology, his eligible female talent pool is international and global. He can pick and choose from countless women. In order to compete and win, you have to be razor sharp in knowing your value, as well as knowing what men view as valuable.

UNDERSTANDING THE CUSTOMER

Many women have a hard time understanding men; it is very difficult and confusing trying to figure them out. How much better would your relationship have been, if you understood your partner better? Men can be walking contradictions, because their words do not always correspond with their actions. A man might say he wants a strong, successful, independent-thinking woman; but when he meets one, he either is intimidated or finds something wrong with her. Then he chooses the woman who is weak, dependent, and highly needy. These kinds of discrepancies and inconsistencies make it hard to understand men.

Nevertheless, it is imperative that you understand the male mind-set, and learn how men think, what they want, and what they do not want. To learn how and what men think, you must know that the male ego is like the Goodyear Blimp. It is big, bloated, and full of hot air; it is very fragile, easily bruised, and slow to heal—so handle with caution. Become familiar with a man's ego, and treat it like a friend.

Here are some insights into the male mind-set and thought process.

1. Men like the thrill of the chase just as much as they enjoy the conquest of the capture. They want to feel the excitement and passion of working for something that they cannot easily have. Men get lazy when they feel secure in the relationship. You must make a man desire you, before he will pursue and fight for you. Play hard to get, but not too hard; if you are easy to get, you are easy to forget.

2. Men have been conditioned and programmed, at an early age, to respond to certain stimuli. They are

stimulated by images and sight, and respond to what they see. This causes them to have a hard time resisting temptation and controlling their primal instincts and desires. Men make assumptions, based upon visually observable qualities. When a man likes what he sees at home, his wandering eyes are less apt to roam. When you dress, highlight your strong points— eyes, chest, derriere, etc. No matter what you have on, always wear confidence, it is a big turn-on.

3. The male brain has the following characteristics: highly systemized, low ability to multitask, high ability to control emotions, low relational orientation, high project orientation, high ability to zone out, tendency to act first and think later when faced with stress, aggressive response to risk, and competitiveness with other males. In addition, men have an aversion to pressure; so try to avoid giving them ultimatums or making them feel like their back is up against the wall. Men will withdraw under stress.

4. Men self-identify according to what they do, what they have done, and what they have; this is how they keep score. The more men have, the better they feel about themselves. They like it when you give them positive feedback on the things they have accomplished or attained. The more you make them feel better about themselves, the better they feel about you.

5. Men are combative and territorial; they don't like to ask for help, information, directions, support, or admit when they are wrong. For a man to admit he is lost or doesn't know something, it is a direct attack on his manhood. Men like to solve problems and fix things. When they can't fix something, it chips away at their masculinity. Men take pride in helping those who depend on them for support. When you suggest something to a man, and then make him feel like it was his own idea, you two will get along just fine. Many men would rather be right than happy. The more you make him feel like he is large and in charge, the more you will get him to do for you what it is you want.

6. Men don't like to talk, and they don't especially want to talk about their feelings. They also have a tendency to discount your feelings. Since childhood, men have been trained to hold back their feelings. Men communicate to report facts, not necessarily to build rapport. Men speak about 12,500 words a day, and women speak about 25,500 words a day. Men don't like the fact that you tell so much of your personal business to other people; they keep so much of theirs locked up inside. Try to minimize the amount of unnecessary talking around men; and when he does share his feelings, let him know you value him opening up to you.

7. Men see in black and white, while women see in color. For men, it's a bottom-line way of thinking and feeling. Men don't want to hear about your labor pains, just show them the baby. If a man asks you what time it is, don't tell him how to make a watch.

8. Men replace sex with intimacy. Men give intimacy to have sex; women have sex, to get intimacy. Don't condition a man to think that intimacy leads to sex; educate him that intimacy is a warm text message that says he misses you, flowers sent to your office, or any visible display of affection. Men don't need a lot of emotional connection to be sexual.

9. Men are naturally competitive. They are taught to be strong and dominant; that's why they like sports, especially the physical ones, like football, boxing, and MMA. Men seek to demonstrate leadership at work, home, and play. Part of his identity is to make his woman think he is the best at everything; it is a mix of innate ego combined with learned narcissism. Allow him to watch ESPN, go to the fitness center, occasionally hang with the boys, and there will be peace in the valley.

WHAT A MAN WANTS FROM A WOMAN

Growing up, I can remember how important it was for me to make sure my mother was happy with me; I would clean the house just to see the smile on her face.

When I played catch in front of the house, I would ask her to watch, so that I could impress her with my skills. When I earned a trophy or a medal, I thought, "This will make my mom proud of me." Men don't ever change in this regard; they still want their mom's approval.

What becomes even more important to a man is his wife/girlfriend's approval. He desperately needs to know that he has the ability to protect her, provide for her, and make her happy.

Most men are concerned with how they are viewed by the significant women in their life. Men are born of a woman, raised by a woman, and it's a woman he goes to for dating, mating, and procreating. Many women don't know, or understand, that their opinion and feelings about their man have a profound effect on his psyche. This level of influence gives her a position of power, and if used intelligently, it could help in creating a loving and lasting relationship.

A man wants four things from his partner in a relationship:

He wants **acceptance.** Accepting him as he is, and not wanting to change him, makes him feel affirmed. Acceptance doesn't mean he thinks that you believe he is perfect; it means you are not trying to change him. A man wants to feel that you think he is wonderful and perfect just like he thinks he is, and no other man could ever fill his shoes. By accepting him, he is more understanding of you and your needs.

He wants **appreciation**. Acknowledging you have received personal benefit, gratification, and value from a man's effort, actions, or behavior makes a man feel appreciated. When a man feels his hard work, kind gesture, or valiant effort was not wasted, he will be encouraged to do more, give more, and try harder. A man who is appreciated feels empowered and motivated to move a mountain to please his woman. Let him know you appreciate his maleness and his manhood.

He wants your **admiration**. A man wants you to admire everything about him, and he needs to hear it in the form of flattery and praise. To admire a man is to regard him with astonishment, delight, and happiness. A man wants to know what you like most about him, what you admire, what makes you proud, what his strengths are, in your eyes. Men never get tired of hearing how wonderful they are.

He wants your **approval**. Men are not complicated. They have simple basic needs, just as women do. When you think a man is wonderful and fabulous, and you let him know you approve of him, you are meeting those needs. A man needs your approval more than you realize. A woman's disapproval can really hurt a man deep inside, and he can carry that hurt for a long time. Be careful with his ego, and think carefully before you let him know you disapprove of him in any way. When a man receives the approval from you that he needs, it becomes easier for him to validate your feelings and meet your needs.

Men primarily want acceptance, appreciation, admiration, approval mixed in with trust and encouragement. Most men will never become emotionally independent enough to affirm themselves. They will always need a woman to validate the fact that they are a good man, who is competent and capable of making you feel safe and secure.

WHAT A MAN WANTS IN A WOMAN

A story: Kristal, at 28 years old, is the newest and youngest lawyer at a moderately sized law firm. Graduating at the top of her class and clerking for a prominent judge, added to an already impressive set of credentials. Single, but tiring of the singles scene, she recently started seeing Henri, a Frenchman, with the alluring accent and European charm. An artist, Henri has been captured and captivated by Kristal's beauty and intellect. Never short of female companionship, Henri has ended two casual relationships he had been in prior to meeting Kristal; for the first time in a long time, he is going to give his all to a single, solitary female.

The reason the 37-year-old painter is willing to upgrade his sole proprietor status for a partnership is because he feels Kristal is worth it. Her gentle spirit, kind heart, and fabulous figure have convinced him that any and everything he would want in a woman, he has in her. What is interesting to Henri is, for the first time, he may be more into a woman than she is into him. Having never been hurt in love, he now is feeling some of the vulnerability of potentially being hurt, which some of his past lovers have felt.

This new and slightly uncomfortable wave of emotion is making him focus and channel all his energies into Kristal. Telling one of his friends in Paris about Kristal, he heard himself use words that he had never used before to describe a woman. He now used words like fluent, intelligent, awesome, patient, alluring, captivating, and sensual. His fellow Parisian was stunned that an American woman had done what no French woman was able to do— capture the heart of Henri Bordeaux.

Henri truly has come to appreciate Kristal's combination of traits, and talents.

It is quite evident that when it comes to what a man wants in a woman, one size won't fit all, and different strokes for different folks; but there are certain qualities, characteristics, and features that men like, which transcend age, race, color, and creed. Here are some universal qualities that all men want their woman to have:

Feminine	Tender	Gentle
Loyal	Attractive	Sensitive
Nurturing	Charming	Funny
Giving	Smart	Sensual
Fit	Patient	Supportive
Understanding	Fair	Sexy

In baseball, there is a term called a "Five-Tool Player"; this is a player who excels at:

1. Hitting for average
2. Hitting for power
3. Base running skills/speed
4. Throwing ability
5. Fielding abilities.

Famous five-tool players have included Willie Mays, Ken Griffey Jr., Barry Bonds, Mickey Mantle, and Alex Rodriguez. When sportswriters refer to them, they usually will say they have the whole package.

When it comes to a woman, most quality men are also looking for the whole package; that whole package is Beauty, Booty, and Brains. Before you rush to judgment and declare me a male chauvinist pig, read my explanation of what it means.

- **Beauty,** to a quality man, is not just a pretty face; it is:
  - A dynamic personality
  - Self-confidence
  - Kind-heartedness

- A caring spirit
- A sincere soul
- An active listener
- A positive attitude
- Generosity with time and talents
- A sense of humor
- Answering to a Higher Power
- An inviting smile
- Being good with children and seniors
- Selflessness.

- **Booty,** to a quality man, is not just a pleasing posterior; it is:
  - Pride in appearance
  - Proportionate shape
  - Good health/fitness
  - Appropriate attire
  - Looking good in clothes
  - Wholesome, everything is natural
  - Jiggling, at a minimum
  - Good posture
  - Sexy gait/walk
  - Fluent movement
  - Graceful gestures
  - Subtly flirtatious
  - Smelling good
  - Well-groomed hair, feet, nails

- **Brainy,** to a quality man, is not just book smarts; it is:
  - Intelligence
  - Good conversation
  - Being well versed on a variety of topics
  - Teaching him new things

- Making him laugh
- Investing in herself
- Desiring to try different things
- Intellectually inquisitive
- Technologically proficient; computer literate
- Well-versed in social media
- Good decision making
- Knowing when to back off
- Slow to anger
- Nonjudgmental
- Knowing there are two sides to a story
- Letting him think it was his idea
- Not being fooled by a handsome face
- Recognizing that everything that glitters isn't gold
- Realizing emotionally available is sometimes better than financially stable.

I hope, when you read what the whole package means, you saw much of yourself in each description. If you feel overwhelmed and think you can't live up to these kinds of expectations, STOP it; that's stinking thinking and won't help you. If there are qualities that you know you can work on, then devise a plan and work on them.

Critical thinking is necessary for accurate self-reflection. You are thinking critically when you use honesty to recognize a flaw, fault, selfish motive, evil intention, or self-deception. When it comes to evaluating yourself on what men are looking for in a woman, and wanting to see how you measure up, you must be open-minded and accept the evidence you might find that would lead you to reassess what your features and benefits are.

WHAT A MAN DOESN'T WANT IN A WOMAN

A story: Kay is a 29-year-old emergency room nurse, who has been dating Simon for one year. She is frustrated, because, in her opinion, Simon is not stepping up and taking the relationship to the next level—which, in her mind, means an engagement ring. In Simon's mind, however, it seems like every day Kay is complaining about what he doesn't do and hasn't done; and he is getting annoyed by it. He believes Kay is not a very happy person, and she takes it out on him.

Kay keeps telling him how great she is, and how he will never find anyone like her, who has her looks, figure, and earning potential.

Simon likes her; but he isn't sure that he could put up with her constant questioning, never-ending phone calls and criticisms, for the rest of his life. He tried to break up with Kay once, and she created such drama, by going to his job, making a scene, and calling his friends to let them know how insensitive and cruel he was being to her. Since going out with Kay, Simon has restricted his male bonding time with his two best friends, Stan and Deon. They don't like Kay, because they see how controlling and demanding she is with their friend. Kay has some abandonment issues, due to her childhood; and subsequently, she smothers Simon by always wanting to be with him. This clingy behavior stems from Kay's fear that Simon is going to dump her. Simon tries to do things to make Kay happy, but she always finds something to complain about and never appreciates his efforts.

Knowing what men want in a woman is important; knowing what men don't want is equally important. Women have been conditioned to focus on what turns a man on; but knowing what turns a man off is also helpful and beneficial, especially when you are in the attraction phase of the dating relationship. Kay's behavior is not helping her relationship with Simon; in fact, it may be causing him to reconsider if there is a long-term future between them.

Here are five traits that Kay displays, which men dislike in a woman:

1. No man likes a woman who is **too clingy.** Kay's refusal to give Simon his personal time and space is pushing him away. At the heart of Kay's clinginess is her insecurity about being dumped. Kay is rarely happy, because she is always worrying about the status of the relationship. If you love someone, you have to let them breathe and not smother them with obsessive phone calling, texting, and wanting to spend all your time with them.

2. No man likes a **complaining** woman. Simon feels all Kay does is complain about what he isn't doing or hasn't done. A complaining partner makes any relationship more complicated than it needs to be, and usually ends in fighting and major disagreements. Try not to be someone who appears to be nagging; make your case, share your opinion, give a solution, and then let it go.

3. Women who are **very demanding** annoy most men, especially when the demands are out of line, unnecessary, and excessive. Simon has 'been committed to Kay and the relationship, but that doesn't mean he enjoys being dictated to on a regular basis. Don't make your partner feel like he is being forced to agree with you or do what you want.

Democracy in a relationship works better than a dictatorship. You get better results at home and at work, when you make someone feel they work with you, rather than for you.

4. Women who **create drama** wear out their welcome real soon. Kay created problems for Simon, when he tried to break off the relationship, which affected both his personal and professional life. Women who major on the minors, make mountains out of molehills, and treat every situation as life and death, will make most men uncomfortable and not want to stick around. Keeping issues and situations in the proper perspective, and the emotional fireworks to a minimum, will help in keeping a man interested.

5. **Controlling** women are a major turn-off for most men. A woman who feels the need to control every aspect of the relationship, and control their partner's every move, will tax the last nerve of even the most patient man. Kay's constant questioning, and limiting of Simon's time with his friends, has caused a strain in the relationship. Grown men don't like to feel like human chess pieces, being positioned, maneuvered, and controlled. Let your partner be part of the decisions that affect the relationship, and make him feel he has a voice in what and where the relationship is going.

Reviewing some of the things that Kay did, which are causing issues in her relationship, is an opportunity to use one of the key skills that an entrepreneur needs to use to be successful in their business endeavor; and that is the skill of self-management.

Talking about traits that men don't like in a woman calls for you to take a look in the mirror. Ask the person staring back, "what are the things that she does that could cause a potential partner to be turned off." This may make you look at yourself in a new light and assess some of your behaviors, attitudes, and actions. Give yourself the time and encouragement to move forward in your pursuit of being the woman who makes her relationship dreams come true.

FIVE THINGS A MAN WANTS BUT WON'T TELL YOU

1. He wants you to keep him challenged, because that keeps him interested; and he knows he gets lazy when he feels secure in the relationship; keep the intrigue and excitement alive.

2. He wants you to tell him you are proud of him. Your endorsement is critical to how he feels about himself. Knowing you have confidence in his competence is like Vitamin E for his ego.

3. He wants you to desire him, physically. He finds you virtually irresistible, when you have the combination of nice and naughty in a confident, classy way. A confident woman is very sexy. A woman who knows her worth, and will not settle for anything less, is a woman worth keeping.

4. He wants to know you are interested in him. Many men are afraid of rejection; so before they jump into the deep end of the dating pool, they would like to have some sign that it's safe.

5. He wants you to make a commitment to him. Most
    men, regardless of popular opinion, are not "dogs"
    who sleep around. Most men want fidelity and a
    woman who can commit wholeheartedly to them.

CUSTOMER SEGMENTS

When I was General Manager at Nike, one of the things that we did was segment our customer base. There were Sporting Goods stores, Department stores, Athletic Specialty stores, Big Box, National accounts, Military, and Strategic accounts. We were able to do this, by looking at factors, such as geographical location, size and type, lifestyle, attitudes, and buying habits of consumers. Segmentation allows you to segment your customers into groups sharing similar needs. This practice helps with the following:

Customizing and improving products and services, to meet each segment's needs.

- Identifying your most and least profitable customers

- Focusing your marketing on the segments most likely to buy your products or services

- Building loyal relationships with customers by developing the products and services they wanted and needed

- Getting ahead of the competition

- Structuring your pricing

- Identifying niche markets (a specific area of your market that may be overlooked by competitors.)

If you were going to open a business, how you segment your customers will depend on whether you market your products to businesses or to individual consumers.

If you are segmenting business markets, you could divide the market by:

- What they do – industry sector, public or private, size and location
  - How they operate – technology, use of your products

  - Their buying patterns – how and when they place orders

  - How they behave – loyalty and attitude to risk.

If you are segmenting consumer markets, you could group customers by:

- Location – towns, regions and countries

- Profiles – such as age, gender, income, occupation, education, social class

- Attitudes – lifestyles

- Buying behavior – including product usage, brand loyalty and the benefits they want from the product or service

Romance like business can be segmented; there is a variety of different types of partners that a woman can select from.

A story: Donna is a 34-year-old clothes designer for an urban clothing line. She is trendy, hip, and very comfortable in her own skin. She never married, but came close three years ago with Ben, a 49-year-old dentist. She felt she loved him, but she was not prepared to give up her career and just be his dutiful wife. That experience made her stay away from older men, because Ben was her second older man. She had a brief, strange relationship with Chester, a 73-year-old retired Air Force colonel. She began dating Casper, a 25-year-old graphic artist; he was focused on growing his career, appreciated Donna's beauty and intellect, but was also interested in adding more names and numbers to his little black book. It ended before much ever got started. Currently, she is dating Mack, a 36-year-old schoolteacher; they enjoy each other's company, seem to be compatible, and share similar values. Mack is very expressive of his feelings toward Donna, and lets her know he loves her femininity, her tenderness, and quiet strength. Donna is optimistic that he might be the one.

Asking what a man wants in a woman is a difficult question to answer, because it's dependent on the man, where he is in his life, and what his expectations are from his partner and the relationship. Like Donna, many women are crossing generational lines when dating; each one of those lines is looking for something different in their partner.

Looking at the four men Donna dated, you see the different generations; and each generation has its own view on dating, monogamy, and marriage. For the first time in this nation's history, we have four generations working under the same roof, at the same time; and their specific business strategies for success differ significantly.

It should then be no surprise that their views and beliefs about personal relationships also differ. Let's segment her four men into four groups: Traditionalists, Baby Boomers, Generation X, and Generation Y, so that we gain some understanding.

Chester – **Traditionalists** – (1927-1945), age 67 and over, population nearly 75 million. This is the "World War II" generation. This marvelous group of people fought and won two world wars, saw the fall of the stock exchange in October 1929, did not have the safety net of social security, welfare, unemployment, health and life insurance, or insurance on their bank deposits. They know how to save. In fact, they hold three-quarters of all financial assets in the United States, and their total net worth is $7 trillion.

Traditionalists are very patriotic, with a significant percentage being veterans of the armed forces. This generation knew how to get things done, despite the odds. They built the space program, landed a man on the moon, created miracle vaccines and antibiotics, wiped out polio, tuberculosis, and the whooping cough. They have a strong work ethic, and believe in the institution and the business of getting things done. This group was loyal to the company and typically retired from the same company after 35 to 40 years.

For this generational group, dating leads to marriage; if you were not married by the age of 30, something was wrong with you. Moreover, when you got married, it was for life. This generation did not believe in, or embrace, divorce; in fact, it was frowned upon.

When you dated, you dated only that man or woman; your life centered around that person and that person only (going steady, getting pinned, getting engaged, and getting married). Dating was supervised, and both sets of parents had to approve of the location, the time, the interaction, and, of course, somebody was with you the entire time. They did not tolerate "hanky panky." A woman who was perceived as "loose," was shipped to a distant relative. A "loose" woman might as well wear a scarlet letter. Sexuality was definitely not a conversation that was appropriate in any venue for women, and you "saved" yourself for marriage.

You can expect a date with a traditionalist to be formal, expect to be picked up, and expect a flower or flowers. He will make dinner reservations, most likely; and he will be punctual and will expect you to be on time, too. He will pay for dinner and expect that you will give him some flexibility in ordering from the menu for the two of you. He will want you to look your best, sexy but not provocative. He will open the car door for you and hold your hand as you get into the car. He will display strong family values. Due to his age, he has experienced loss and death in his life; it could be a wife, a child, a best friend, or his parents (one or both). He may or may not be retired. He will most likely have grandchildren, and he will be set in his ways. He may not share a lot of information with you on the first date. Don't be Talkative Tina, but rather Casual Conversation Cathy. Don't tell all of your business. By all means, don't cut him off while he is speaking, and don't outdo his accomplishments with your own. Compliment his accomplishments and his commitment and dedication to his country, if he is a veteran. He is strictly in a Corporation (marriage) mode.

Ben – **Baby Boomers** – (1946-1964), age 48 to 66, population 80 million. This generation enjoyed a booming birthrate (dad came home from the war) and economic prosperity. The traditionalists cherished and loved them, and spoiled them rotten. This competitive generation experienced the civil rights movement, television, women's liberation, Watergate, assassinations, and Vietnam. This group spends more than it saves. They trend everything from jeans to cars to titles. They are an optimistic generation and see the possibilities in everything they touch, see, or experience. They wanted to change everything and be the first. They are the largest generation in the history of this country, so competition is keen among them. This generation is also known as "workaholics" and typically put their careers first. Boomers also were identified with sex, drugs, and rock and roll.

Baby boomers made history in going out and "hooking up." First and foremost, they changed the ritualistic dating standards of the Traditionalists, thanks to the women's movement. Going Dutch (splitting the check) became acceptable and the divorce rate soared to three times higher than any previous generation. They rebelled against the philosophy of "chaperoning." *The Dating Game,* premiered on television; and women looked to Mary Richards, the working girl portrayed on *The Mary Tyler Moore Show*, as a role model. Sex before marriage was common, because birth control pills eliminated the fear of pregnancy; and having sex in many different places, including the mile high club (in bathrooms on airplanes), was considered fun.

Shacking up, or living together before marriage, came on the scene; and co-ed facilities in colleges/universities and some aspects of the military came about. Having more than one partner to date was okay, and having more than one partner sexually was not seen to be unusual. Baby Boomer men love sexy women, who are 10 to 20 years younger. Regardless, if he has kept in shape, he wants his woman to be fine, fit, and frisky. Boomers don't care for the new wave of heavy makeup, false eyelashes, unnatural-looking wigs, and finger-long fingernails. Natural is better, but if you must add to your appearance, make sure it is tasteful.

Baby boomer men are mature, and they know what they want in a woman and in a relationship. If the first date does not give them that "warm and fuzzy" feeling, you won't have to worry about a second date, or even a follow-up call. They expect you to know who you are and what you need in a relationship. Why? You are mature adults; there is no time for game playing or lack of confidence. Now, a word of advice: don't just look for anyone, because you are desperate or lonely; take your time. Focus on being attractive, look for someone with similar interests, go to places where you feel safe, consider online dating, watch out for rebound relationships, and know that health problems may be a factor. Baby boomer men don't mind you flirting with them a little. Have fun and don't talk about or mention your ex. Let him feel that he is king, at least for a day. Boomers are often called arrogant, because they flaunt their material possessions or professional status. The trouble the baby boomer man runs into is: if he dates a woman too young she wants kids, and that's a deal breaker. If he dates a career woman, she won't give him her undivided attention, and that's a deal breaker.

If he dates a woman his own age or older, she might not meet his physical requirements, and that's a deal breaker. You would think he would be in a Corporation mode or at worst in a Partnership (relationship) mode, but too many times, he acts like a Sole Proprietor (single looking to mingle).

Mack – **Generation X** – (1965-1980), age 30 to 47, population 46 million, is the generation that is more skeptical and questions everything. They were influenced, very early in their lives, by divorce, missing children on milk cartons, AIDS, cable television, personal computers, Sesame Street, and being latchkey children. This is a generation that believes in flexibility of schedules, informal structures and dress codes, strong sense of family values, quality of life, entrepreneurship, resourcefulness, and being highly adaptive to change. They do not live to work; they work to live. Cell phones appeared on the scene for this generation, along with major malls, transportation, and internet dating.

The Generation X approaches to dating and marriage is complex. Men and women have fewer expectations to live up to relationship-wise. In fact, they tend to be more skeptical about whom they are "hooking up" with than the hook-up itself. This generation values communication, honesty, and truth. Nothing is worse than lying to a skeptic. There is no hesitation to "drop you" like a hot potato and move on to someone else. Generation X men do not like to be told what to do, nor do they like for a woman to be bossy or authoritative.

Dating does not have to be formal or governed by set times, standards, or schedules. A date might be a sporting activity or event, where dressing casually in jeans is okay.

When dating in this generation, keep your expectations realistic and your mind open. Going Dutch is okay, and even paying for the meal is cool. If you want to invite him out, call him. This generation is also very sensitive to the environment and a healthy lifestyle. Your date could be doing something to help the environment or working out at the gym. The point is, expect the unexpected and don't be afraid to try new and different things that are safe. This generation of man prefers women 5 to 10 years younger. He is at an age where the wild oats have been sowed, and he is now looking to be stable and settled. When he dates, he is looking at a woman and measuring her wife and mother potential. He is a Partnership and would be willing to go to the LLC (cohabitation) route; but in his heart, he is a Corporation waiting to happen.

Casper – **Generation Y** – (1981-2000), 30 and younger, 75 million strong. This techno-savvy, diverse, energetic, safety-conscious, collaborative, street-smart, and confident generation is changing all of the rules, as they enter the world of work with high expectations of success. Their bright disposition and gleaming hope for the future is encouraging, in spite of gang violence, school shootings, and international and domestic terrorism pervading their young lives. Already, this multitasking generation is the most educated generation of any in our history, and their views on dating and marriage are more radically different than we ever thought possible. Generation Y openly embraces interracial dating and marriage, gay dating and marriage, and waiting until later in life to get married. Their circle of friends and sphere of influence is diverse and multicultural.

While they believe in the institution of marriage, waiting is what they prefer to do; first, they have to see the world, conquer it, and figure out what's next. They believe strongly in family and in celebrating life to the fullest. Want to live together? No problem, but pay your way. Want to date? No problem, pay your way, and mine, too, if you want. Be fashionable, and understand that texting will occur before phone calls.

Social media is the norm. Don't be surprised if the results of your date—or how he feels about the date—end up on Facebook or Twitter, and pictures show up on Instagram. This generational man prefers women a year or two younger; but since the "Cougar" phenomenon, they too are walking on the generational wild side. This laid-back, Renaissance man wannabe enjoys and appreciates a woman's intellect, beauty, and sexuality. Though he relishes the getting to know you phase of dating, he is very focused on establishing his career and trying to make his mark on the world .As much as you think he is captivated by your company, which he probably is, he also enjoys the company of other women. He is a Sole Proprietor and not looking to change status any time soon.

Regardless of the generation you choose to date, the most important thing is just be you.

UNDERSTANDING THE COMPETITION
(OTHER SINGLE WOMEN)

When you are doing a competitive analysis, you need to identify your competition by product line or service, as well as by market segment; assess their strengths and weaknesses, determine how important your target market is to your competitors, and identify any barriers that may hinder you as you are entering the market.

A story: Fiona, a 41-year-old advertising executive for a major agency, has not been in a relationship for years; she refers to herself as a serial dater. The nature of her business has her in the party scene, because her largest client is in the distilled spirits industry. Moderately attractive, but quite outgoing, Fiona is often accused of being flirty. Her confidence and decisiveness intimidates both men and women. Recently, she saw a former co-worker enter a club with a strikingly handsome hunk of a man. When she walked up to say hello, it was apparent that Eric, the hunk, was equally as interested in her, because he couldn't take his eyes off of her cleavage; not wanting to be too obvious, she left the couple. The thought of this man at her side and in her bed got Fiona's intellectual and feminine juices flowing. She asked a male friend of hers to follow her new heart's desire into the restroom, and ask for his cell-phone number, on her behalf. Upon leaving the club, he gave her a glance, which she interpreted to mean, I cannot wait for you to call me. Three months later, Fiona and Eric are a couple. There was no shame to her game. She saw what she wanted and didn't care whom he belonged to; she claimed him for her own. Was Fiona a vamp or a champ?

If you don't have a friend like Fiona, or know someone like Fiona, you will soon, because they are out there and more are coming. Today's social structure is telling women that they must constantly compete with each other, that competition is not just for the boardroom but also for the bedroom. Fiona had little or no regard for what belonged to another woman, and this attitude is prevalent among many single women.

Gender expert Susan Shapiro Barash is a professor of critical thinking and gender studies at Marymount Manhattan College in New York. She interviewed 500 women in the United States, and forty percent of them said another woman had stolen their boyfriend, lover, husband or job at some time in their lives. Twenty-five percent admitted they have done the stealing as well. That's not the half of it; according to Barash's research and interviews with these women, here's what else they said:

- Ninety percent admit they are (or have been) envious and jealous of other women in their lives.

- Sixty-five percent say they feel that way (envious and jealous) about their sister or best friend.

- Eighty percent say they have been victims of another woman's envy or jealousy.

- Ninety percent of women say the toughest workplace competition comes from women, not men.

Barash says that rivalry is part of the human condition for women, and it starts at a very young age. "By sixth grade, we know who the popular, pretty, sporty, brainy girls are. And we spend the rest of our lives working with these stereotypes, being part of it, and being very jealous of what we don't have," Barash said. She goes on to say it's a rivalry that is uniquely female—pitting woman against woman, girl against girlfriend, sister against sister, mother against daughter, and vice versa.

Relationship economics says it's a jungle out there in the single world, and only the strong will thrive. Much of what makes it a jungle is the theory of scarcity, which we discussed in Chapter 5. Scarcity creates the supply and demand dilemma. When there is a high demand and a limited supply, the price goes up. Price is the effort and energy a woman will invest in finding a partner. "Because of the scarcity of goods," Barash says, "We [women] are taught winner takes all—the sense that there is only one [glass] slipper, one crown; and therefore, if she has it, I cannot have it.

As a successful, sassy, single woman with a lot going for herself, if you can't or don't effectively differentiate yourself from the other successful, sassy, single women in the mind of your target market (single men), it's going to be difficult to find the right man. If you don't talk, walk, think, act differently or better than the competition, then you won't stand out and rise above the competitive clutter.

Here's what the competition looks like:

- The average American woman is 38.2 years of age.

- The average American woman is 5 feet, 4 inches tall.
- The average American woman weighs 164 pounds.

- The average American model is 5 feet, 11 inches tall, and weighs 117 pounds.

- Most fashion models are thinner than 98 percent of American women.

- Four out of five American women say they are dissatisfied with the way they look.

- On any given day, almost half of the women in the United States are on a diet.

- The average age for American women to get married in the U.S. is 27.

- In 2010, the median weekly earnings of full-time working women was $669, compared to $824 for men.

- The median annual income for full-time, year-round women workers in 2009 was $36,278, compared to men's $47,127.

- In 2010, the median weekly earnings for women in full-time management, professional, and related occupations was $923, compared to $1,256 for men.

- In 2009, full-time working married women with spouses present had median usual weekly earnings of $708, somewhat higher than never married women ($577) or women of other marital status (divorced, separated, or widowed – $646).

- In 2009, Asian women, who were full-time wage and salary workers, had higher median weekly earnings than women of all other races/ethnicities, as well as African-American and Latino men.

Education is a factor in income – statistics show that higher degrees lead to higher median salaries. For full-time workers data below, men earn more than women in each category.

Degree	Median weekly earnings, women	Median weekly earnings, men
Doctoral	$1,243	$1,754
Professional	$1,269	$1,772
Master's	$1,126	$1,458
Bachelor's	$891	$1,200
Associate's	$674	$878
High school graduate, no college	$542	$716

Bureau of Labor Statistics, Current Population Survey, "Table 17: Median Usual Weekly Earnings of Full-time Wage and Salary Workers 25 Years and Over by Educational Attainment and Sex," 2009 Annual Averages, *Women in the Labor Force: A Data book* (2010 Edition)

A story: Heather is a 38-year-old entrepreneur, who has started four different businesses. The first three were not financially successful, but her new business, Maids on Wheels, is turning out to be quite profitable. After graduating from college, Heather refused to work for anyone other than herself, borrowing $1,200 from a group of four friends, she started her first business, a professional dog-walking service. She made money but stopped enjoying it, so she shut it down. With no capital or collateral, she walked into her local bank, met with the manager, and secured a $2,000 loan, to start a tutoring business specializing in the STEM subjects—Science, Technology, Engineering, and Math.

After two years, and a major health scare, she shut the business down. In between all of her entrepreneurial pursuits, Heather found the time to have a relationship with Oscar, who didn't turn out to be what she expected. He turned out to be on the down-low. She was honest with him; she said she couldn't deal with the idea of her man liking the same thing that she liked in the bedroom. Her next venture was an escort service with a twist, she paired widows and widowers. This brought her peace and joy, but she got out of it when one of her female clients sued her, because she was stalked by one of her sponsored escorts. During the time span of her escort business closing, and her Maid on Wheels business opening, she got engaged to Kendall, a college classmate whom she hadn't seen in three years. They met the night she turned down Oscar's attempt to win her back, by declaring himself 100 percent heterosexual, after he went to counseling. Kendall was in the same restaurant that evening; and from that night on, they have been virtually inseparable, and she has never been happier.

Looking at the competitive landscape, Heather is the prototypical woman with whom you are competing. She has the kind of qualities that successful women have today, which affords them a chance to achieve many of their goals and aspirations. Let's look at seven traits of today's successful woman:

- **Ambition:** Drive and hard work are admirable qualities and are useful in business and in romance. Heather always had a vision and a goal and was not afraid to dream big. Often, in corporate America, an ambitious woman is wrongfully labeled as being too masculine, when the same trait in men is rewarded.

- **Determination:** With any entrepreneur, it's no risk, no reward. Heather was not afraid of failure; and her ability to try again, again, and again is her greatest strength. A determined woman is tough to compete against on any level.

- **Resourcefulness:** In order to get where you want to go, sometimes you have to make detours, find alternative routes, and use every tool in your bag of tricks. Skill, combined with will, is a combination that usually crosses the finish line first. Heather used all the resources at her disposal to make things happen

- **Intelligence:** The modern woman must have a double dose of book smarts and street smarts, to be able to know the diamonds from the zirconium, and realize that everything that glitters isn't gold. Heather was able to discern things about Oscar that led her to cut him loose and minimize her costs.

- **Confidence.** If you don't believe in yourself, who will? Today's woman must market herself as an asset. She must let the world know, and the man of her choice know, what value she offers. Heather was confident enough to walk in the bank with nothing, and leave with a loan.

- **Passion:** You must have viewpoints and ideas and be able to share them and defend them, when necessary. Passion, fused with determination, is a knockout punch to most things that would stand in your way. Heather is passionate about being an entrepreneur and loves the challenges and the triumphs.

- **People skills:** Individuals, who know how to communicate with people and have a genuine like for them, usually have the support of whomever they come in contact with. Women who use the "Platinum Rule," which is treat people the way **they** want to be treated, go far in life and business. Heather is fair and firm, and most people respond to that form of treatment very well.

Which of these traits could you improve on, and why?

_____

_____

_____

_____

COMPETITIVE SEGMENTS
They say all is fair in love and war, so you never know against whom you may compete. It is important to understand the characteristics and traits of all the generational women.

Traditionalists – (1927-1945)
These ladies are retired from the workforce, or near retirement. They have a strong work ethic, because they grew up during lean times and consider work a privilege. To her, education was a dream. This generation believes you earn your own way through hard work. She is civic-minded and loyal to her country and employer; chances are she worked for the same employer her entire life. She communicates by rotary phone, one-on-one conversations, or through memos. Men like her,

because she is submissive and generally doesn't like to ruffle any feathers or initiate any conflict. Because she was raised in a paternalistic environment, she respects authority. She saves her money and pays cash for everything. Slow to change, she has not adjusted to technology very well. This woman values morals, safety, security, conformity, consistency, and commitment.

Baby Boomers – (1946-1964)

These ladies are well-established in their careers, and hold positions of power and authority. Nearly 80 million will exit the workplace in the next decade; they are retiring at the rate of 8,000 per day, or more than 300 per hour. To her, education was a birthright. She is motivated by positions, perks, and prestige; and she defines herself by her professional accomplishments. Many would consider her a workaholic. She believes the younger generation has not paid their dues in the workplace. She communicates by cell phone, and says you can call her anytime.

Men sometimes are intimidated, because she is independent, confident, and self-reliant. She believes in buying things now and paying for them later. This is a formidable opponent, because she is educated, financially secure, dedicated, focused, and thinks that if she can't change the world, she surely will make a difference. If you tangle with her, remember she is clever, resourceful, and hates to lose at anything.

Generation X- (1965-1980)

These ladies are educated, ethnically diverse, and have not had opportunities to move into management in the workplace, because a baby boomer is still there. She is individualistic, resourceful, and self-sufficient. She might be this way because she was a latchkey kid. To her, education is the ticket to get where she wants to go. She displays a subtle disdain for authority and structured work hours. She likes to be managed by being left alone; she despises micromanagers. She is not committed to one employer, and will willingly move to change jobs to get ahead. She communicates by IPhones BlackBerry, e-mail, and laptop; she is also technically adept Men like her because she is fun. She is conservative with her money; this girl is a saver. She adapts well to change and appreciates diversity and alternative lifestyles. She is ambitious and eager to learn new things, but she wants success on her own terms.

Generation Y – (1981-2000)

These ladies have either been underemployed, working part-time, or out of work during the recession. It is very unlikely that she will stay with her current employer for the remainder of her working life; she probably has already switched careers once.

Education to her was a terrible expense, and she is drowning in student-loan debt. This lady is entrepreneurial, very goal-oriented, and is good at multitasking.

She communicates by texting, voicemail, blogging, or tweeting; she is very proficient with technology. She has created a profile on a social networking site. She probably is struggling to pay her bills; she has more than three credit cards, and all are near the limit. She may be living at home or thinking about moving back in; she is receiving financial support from her parents, so that she can make ends meet. Whatever money she makes, she spends; saving is an odd concept. Men like her because she is quite social, oozes confidence, and has few inhibitions. She works well in teams and likes to work with other creative people.

WHERE TO FIND THE MARKET

In business, the challenge was always looking for new customers. When people used to ask me how to do it, I would ask them this question, "In order to catch fish, what do you need to do?" They would respond "...use the right bait, have a pole, etc." The answer is, "You have to fish where the fish are." That is the answer that I would give to the question "How do you find a quality man? You have to go where the men are. Knowing where the quality men are is not always easy for the successful, sassy, single woman. Here is my question to you: Were you in the right place but had the wrong bait (ability to get their attention), or were you in the wrong place but had the right bait? The answer to these questions would determine what strategy you need to employ. Therefore, we have two separate issues, where do I go to find men, and how do I get their attention?

Are you are looking for that limited commodity (dream man), which for most women means a 10? Remember two key things: 1) dream men aren't out a lot, because dating isn't something they struggle with; and 2) if you are out 10-hunting, you need to be close to a 10, yourself, or he isn't going to approach you or allow you to approach him.

Here are 10 Places to look for your mate:

1. **A golf course:** Golf links are not only where men are, but where professional men are. Many a business deal has been transacted while golfing. I have always recommended to young professionals, both male and female, to take up golf, because it will give you a great opportunity to build your network. If you want attention, go to a driving range and look like you need help with your swing. You will be overwhelmed with the number of male volunteers willing to help you. If I meet a woman who likes golf, and likes to golf, she immediately gets brownie points.

2. **Sport bars:** High-end sports bars will never have a shortage of men, especially on a game day. Going alone, or with girlfriends, will normally get you noticed. The noise sometimes can be distracting, but it's a good opportunity to observe someone you might be interested in and develop a game plan to get their attention.

3. **Charity events:** Successful men usually gather at these kinds of events. Depending on the event, a potential drawback might be that your dream man has a date; but don't despair, because it could have been arranged and there is no true love connection; so feel free to engage in conversation.

4. **Self-improvement workshops:** Go to one that you could really use to improve yourself; you don't want to make up an addiction or malady just to find a partner. The caring environment will help you decide who is kind and considerate or who is certifiably troubled.

5. **Sporting events:** There is never a shortage of men at a sporting event. When you attend an event, and you present yourself well, you will get male attention. You have to make yourself available at halftime, or at a lull in the action, so that someone would feel comfortable to approach you without taking away from the game or match.

6. **Spa resort:** Most of these types of facilities have a fancy clientele, so the chances of meeting a high-caliber individual is high; however, a drawback

might be that there are not many of them there on the day that you are there.

7. **Premieres and parties:** Not always an easy ticket or invitation; but if you can score one, you are rubbing elbows with 10's and, probably, no less than strong 8's. In events like this, you have to have your portable B.S. detector, because a lot of never-beens and wannabes parade around as big shots.

8. **Fashionable pubs:** Many successful men frequent the local watering hole near their place of work. Once you identify such a location, an attractive woman dining alone will catch the eye of most single men and, unfortunately, a few married men, too.

9. **Local health store:** You know one thing; he is health-minded. Most of these places have a spot where they allow you to hang a flyer, so you can find out about upcoming events. Walking an aisle, looking at the products and reading the labels, will catch the eye of mister soymilk. These aisles are the new produce section of the grocery store, where you were once waiting for mister man to squeeze your melons.

10. **Coffee bars:** This one I have heard about more than I have frequented myself, because I don't drink coffee; but one thing I do know is that there seems to be something aphrodisiac-like about the smell of those coffee beans. Take a seat, look lonely, and maybe mister man will come over to see what's percolating.

Here is a list of other potential places you can find your partner. Circle the ones you think will work for you.

The Bar	Newspapers	House Party
The Supermarket	Favorite Restaurant	Book Club
Online	College- Taking Classes	Blood Drive
Church	Walking Your Dog	Art Exhibits
Workplace	Acting Workshops	Wine Tasting
Friends	Ski Resort	Running Club
Gym	Armed Services	Weddings
Vacation Spot	Bowling Alley	Dance Class
Parks	Skating Rink	Laundromats
Airplane	Sushi Bar	Jury Duty
Music Concert	The Beach	Casinos
Cigar Bar	The Bookstore	Museums
Networking Event	Hardware Store	Tech Store

List the places you circled.

_____

_____

_____

_____

_____

Now you know where the future man in your life goes; how do you get him to go for you? Here are five things you can do.

1. **Bare your body:** Dress so that he knows what you are working with. If you need to spend more time in the gym to tighten a few things up, take the time to do it; because if you don't turn his head the first time, there may not be a second chance. You never get a second chance to make a first impression.

2. **Dress "sharp":** An impressive wardrobe will catch the eye of a quality man. Try to be seductive, without working it too hard. Leave some things to the imagination, but don't be afraid to put something on his mind. There are few things sexier than a classy woman in a classy outfit.

3. **Smile:** Nothing lights up a room more than a warm smile looking my way. A smile tells me a lot about what a woman thinks of herself. A smile spells confidence, and to me confidence smells sexy. A smile aimed in my direction will capture my

attention. I like it when I catch you looking at me, smiling.

4. **Touching:** During casual conversation, if you touch my arm or hand in a kind way, you just got my attention. Tactile stimulation is a nice way to say you are interested.

5. **Sell you:** As a former salesman, I can appreciate when someone knows their product and hits me with the features and the benefits. Knowing your value and worth, and being able to articulate it without coming across as arrogant, is quite attention holding.

CHAPTER FOURTEEN
THE PLAN

THE 4 P'S

It's important to realize in the journey of finding a partner that you can't attract everyone, and everyone is not going to be attracted to you. This marketing fact of life, makes having a strategic plan critical in providing direction for how you will channel your effort and energy in finding, attracting, and retaining the right man.

The Plan is a strategic tool to assist you in preparing the "path" for your journey; it focuses on the 4 P's which are the Past, Present, Partner, and Partnership. The Plan helps by reviewing and learning from the past, preparing and planning for the present while anticipating and positioning for the future.

PAST: In order to intelligently move forward sometimes you have to look back; to learn what worked, what didn't and what will you do differently. Analyzing past partners and past relationships help you learn valuable lessons and turn them into positive reinforcements. You sometimes realize in relationships you were either the powerful one or the vulnerable one; through empowerment you allow yourself to be truly who you are, which may mean being both powerful and vulnerable depending on the situation; but you should never be unwise.

When you identify mistakes and harmful patterns of behavior from past relationships; learn to recognize the signs and not repeat those negative actions.

Some actions or habits need to be stopped, while others need to be practiced and improved.

In order for your next relationship to start fresh you must forgive yourself and have healed from any hurt, pain, or ill-feeling caused by a previous partner. Stop punishing yourself for failed relationships. Don't get bitter, get better; bitter fruit bears bitter juice.

Believe in the powers of romantic possibilities, stay positive with your thoughts, actions, and words and rather than focusing on what didn't work in your relationships, remember what was right and what did work.

Here are 5 things that may prevent you from making romantic mistakes.

1. Be fully recovered from the previous relationship; let go of any misgivings, guilt, shame, resentment, and self-pity you may still have before entering a new relationship.

2. Don't confuse chemistry with compatibility. In business, decisions are made using reason, being rational, and focusing on the facts. You don't make business decisions based on emotion. Compatibility is based on facts; chemistry is based on emotion.

3. Don't confuse attraction with acceptance. Just because you seem to attract a certain type of partner does not mean you have to accept them into your life. Everything that looks good to you might not be good for you. It takes months of talking to learn about a person's history. Do your due diligences

before you accept a partner and let them share your air.

4. Don't make them a priority, if they make you an option. Don't make yourself to available to someone who isn't interested in a committed relationship. If you are a Partnership, LLC or Corporation don't get involved with a Sole Proprietor.

5. You must have the crucial conversation with a partner to know if you both are wanting a relationship and what that means; commitment, monogamy, and exclusivity.

PRESENT: No matter where you are in your personal or romantic life, there is always room for improvement. There are many ways in which to improve your life and create positive change. In order to achieve your vision and goals you must recognize what's holding you back and overcome those obstacles. Focus on all the good things in your life and remove all of the **ANTS** (Automatic Negative Thoughts) that distract and discourage you. Negative thoughts are a complete waste of time and energy and if you don't eliminate them you can sabotage your success.

The more you find out about yourself and express your authentic self, the more meaning, joy and fulfillment you will have in your life. Many of the assessment questions should have helped you understand yourself better personally and romantically.

When it comes to romantic relationships analyze the following about you:

- **Strengths**- What do you do well?

- **Weaknesses**- What could you improve?

- **Opportunities**- What partner prospects do you have?

- **Threats**- What people or situations could harm you?

To effectively work in the present you have to be at peace with who you are, what you stand for, and what you want from a partner and a relationship. Knowing your needs, your boundaries, and your non-negotiable standards of behavior will make the road to finding a quality partner and having a healthy relationship smoother with fewer obstacles and barriers.

PARTNER: Finding, attracting, and retaining the right partner is about knowing what you want, knowing what you don't what, knowing who you are looking for, knowing where you might find them, and then getting and keeping their attention.

You have identified what characteristics you want in a quality partner but have you identified other specifications or qualifications? The better you are at narrowing down what you want in a partner the easier it will be to identify it; as well as knowing who it isn't. As a successful sassy single woman you have the power to choose your mate. You can choose someone who is fully developed or one who is still developing. You know you shouldn't be fooled by the outward appearance of a person; you must look underneath and see the true person. Reviewing your past partners you should have identified if it appears you consistently fall for a certain kind of man. Here is a list of a few types; see if you seem to be attracted to any particular one.

- **The Thug-** fun and exciting, will protect you, always drama, drinks too much

- **The Intellectual-** cares about your feelings, has good job, boring, not street smart

- **The Playa-** tells you he sees other women, good lover, doesn't acknowledge you in public, usually is a punk, and wants you to believe his lies.

- **The Romantic-** brings flowers, calls often, shares his feelings, in love with the idea of love, comes on strong but loses momentum

- **The Sexy Older Man-** lifetime of experience in and out of bed, wise, stable, health problems, slow pace, not a lot of fun

- **The Cool One-** secure in himself, assertive, aware he has it going on, not always supportive of you, usually is busy because his dance card is full.

- **The Bad Boy-** a bit of a rebel, carefree attitude, you want to tame him, you know he isn't good for you but he is so much fun

- **The Quality One-** respects women, loves his mother, treats you nice, he is in demand, can't say no, nice career, he will do right by you.

Maybe you attract these types of men:

- **Mr. Needy**- insecure, dependent, needs constant reassurance, doubts himself

- **Mr. Predictable**- you know his every reaction, set in his ways, won't do anything different,

- **Mr. Arrogant**- huge ego, condescending, rude to others he thinks are below him .

- **Mr. Cheapo**- suggest you go dutch, has the first dollar he ever made, is penny wise and pound foolish

- **Mr. Argumentative**- turns every conversation into an argument, makes you feel you are in debate class

- **Mr. Holy-Than-Though**- judgmental of others, sometimes so heavenly minded he is no earthly good.

- **Mr. I Don't Like Women**- bitter towards women, makes rude insulting comments

- **Mr. Immature**- spoiled as a child, avoids responsibility, doesn't feel the need to please women, very egotistical

- **Mr. Ambitious**- strong will, wants to prove himself, very masculine, has achieved a lot

In looking for the right man it helps considerably if you know what your preference is concerning age, annual income, educational level, type of occupation, region of the country you want them to live in, children or not, home owner, lifestyle, behaviors, and attitude. The more you know about the man you want; the better chance you have to find him.

PARTNERSHIP: A partnership is a relationship between individuals that is characterized by mutual cooperation and responsibility, for the achievement of a specified goal. For many that goal is marriage; ninety percent of all adults in America marry at some point in their lives. Fifty percent of these marriages end in divorce. This high rate of failure should tell partners in a relationship they have to build strong foundations for a healthy and loving partnership and abide by and encourage the development of key essential and supporting traits that are critical to the relationship's long-term success. Working together with your partner on the process of inserting key traits into the HEART of your relationship on a daily basis will help in developing a strong and lasting bond that goes beyond just plain attraction and intimacy.

The HEART of your partnership is represented by these traits:

- **H**onesty- Build honesty within your relationship in ways that encourage open communication. Agree with your partner today that you will be honest with each other at all times – even if the consequences may somewhat hurt the other person.

Agree that you will always keep an open mind and work through situations in ways that are supportive of your long-term relationship objectives and goals. Always come from the perspective that. It is better to be honest and upfront now, than for your partner to find out later that you were hiding something from them.

- **E**ffective Communication- Communication is a two way street; of primary importance is listening. When your partner is communicating with you be sure to listen with an open mind, with no interruptions and be very attentive to the words they say, the tone of voice they use and to your partner's changing facial expressions throughout their communication. Within these observations you will find clues towards how they are feeling, what perspectives and beliefs they hold, and you will also gain a clear insight into the needs they are attempting to satisfy within this moment. When two people can communicate and share feelings it makes it easier to work through the difficult times.

- **A**dventure- To continue to have intimacy, romance, and passion in a relationship you must do things to keep it alive. Men never want to be bored in their relationships or have it be so predictable they take you for granted; adventurous women are never boring. The trick is to show him that you're open to new experiences and willing to step out of your comfort zone. Keep him wondering, what will she do next.

- **R**espect-To have respect in relationship means to be able to value each other, and understand to accept each other wholly by who you are, and not by what you are. Respect takes many forms here are some things that will demonstrate respect for both your partner and the relationship: 1) acknowledge your partner's contributions to the relationship, 2) honor personal boundaries, 3) be willing to compromise, 4) admit when you are wrong, 5) protect your partner, and 6) show consideration.

- **T**rust- Trust is the foundation for intimate, secure and successful relationships. It must be earned and maintained with consistent actions. Being open with one another builds trust within a relationship and promotes a sense of peace and serenity. Trust has to be a living, breathing entity in order for a relationship to survive.

Every relationship must have shared goals, beliefs and values that synergize perspectives and actions and move you and your partner towards a certain direction with clear, concise and precise objectives.

IT'S NOW UP TO YOU

Writing this book was a labor of love. I wrote it with the motive to help my daughters and other women to find a man who is right for them. While sharing my insights, observations, and points of view I have had one singular goal, to be helpful and to make you think about who you are, what you want out of life, what you want and need from a man, and what it takes to have a loving and lasting relationship.

I wanted this book to help you find out what standards you stand for as a person, what values you stand on as a woman, and what qualities make you stand out as a partner.

I am proud to say that my oldest daughter using principles in this book found her right man and is happily engaged; my youngest daughter is also using the principles and is in a committed relationship. The principles and practices in this book work, but it's now up to you to implement them.

Many of us just needed someone to believe in us at a time we didn't believe in our self. I want you to know I believe you can and will make your relationship dreams come true.

Go forth and prosper knowing that you have The Right Man Business Plan.

About The Author —
RONALD WILLIAMS

With more than thirty years of public and private sector experience under his cincture, it is no surprise that Ronald Williams is one of the most sought after and internationally recognized speakers and trainers in his industry. He goes beyond simply talking at his audience, to ensure that they are both informed and stimulated. He presents information through his high-energy and highly interactive methods of 'edutainment'; which allows him to avoid siphoning the fun and entertainment out of the learning process. Ron's insights on 21st century leadership, employee engagement, customer loyalty development, succession management, and strategic alignment make him one of the nation's leading resources in understanding the success and achievement of today's organizations and individuals.

Currently, he is President of the Brand Enhancing Strategy Team, a training and development company that specializes in the art of B.E.S.T. practices in leadership/management development, team building, and executive coaching. Williams' true passion lies in the realm of relationships, and he is using his knack for making sound business decisions as well as his own personal experiences in order to help single women everywhere learn how to make better, more informed relationship choices.

 @RonWilliamsLive